SECRET
NEW YORK
CURIOUS ACTIVITIES

T. M. Rives

JonGlez

During the research for *Secret New York: An Unusual Guide*, certain entries stood out as more than just places. They unfolded over time, and required a little more effort and attention—in short, they were experiences. It seemed there should be a whole book of such experiences, a map to the oddities and adventures that the city doesn't readily advertise. The result is *Secret New York: Curious Activities*.

"Curious" applies as much to the activities as to the one who seeks them out: a lifelong New Yorker, a wide-eyed tourist, and sojourner from another land, perhaps yourself. Anyone with a willingness to explore and an antenna tuned to the strange. To enjoy *Curious Activities*, find a comfortable chair. To *really* enjoy it, you might want to get out, and move your body, and test your agility and wit, and delight your eyes and ears. It will help if you have a touch with public transportation, or bikes, or boats. Study a map of the five boroughs. Bring a camera. And a notebook. And a pal. Maybe a helmet.

Comments on this guidebook and its contents, as well as information on places we may not have mentioned, are more than welcome and will enrich future editions.

Don't hesitate to contact us:
• Jonglez Publishing, 17, boulevard du Roi,
   78000 Versailles, France
• E-mail: info@jonglezpublishing.com

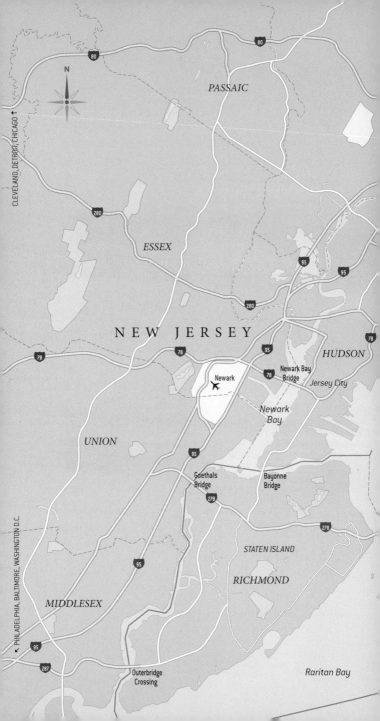

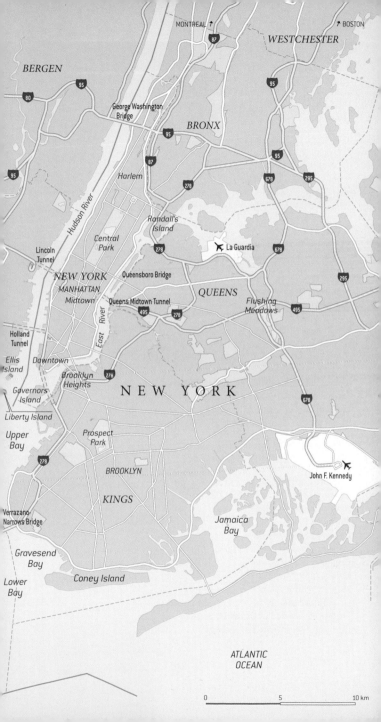

CONTENTS

THRILLS

ARTS / PERFORMANCE

ESCAPE

CONTENTS

NEW SKILL

WESTSIDE RIFLE AND PISTOL RANGE ❶

20 West 20th Street
• www.westsidepistolrange.com
• 212.929.7287
• Transport: N, R, F, M and 6 trains/23 St

Deadly force on Fifth Avenue

Like much of what counts as curious in New York City, the Westside Rifle and Pistol Range owes a lot to location. First, the city itself. In New York it is next to impossible for a citizen to legally own a firearm. On streets where the people are so densely packed, and where some of them take to screaming at trashcans and invisible devils and whatnot, this is a good thing. The range itself is in the basement of a twelve-story building with fancy stone and iron balconies that stands just a couple of blocks south of Madison Square Park. When you open the back door of the polished lobby and hit the stairs, you can already hear the *pow, pow* of guns. A second ago you were walking down Fifth Avenue; now you're among folks with a thing for deadly force. It's a little surreal.

The inside is not too concerned with charm: there's a decided man's touch. Linoleum, walls of institutional green, and a pungent coffee pot. In the hall hangs a photo of Robert De Niro as the well-meaning madman from *Taxi Driver*. It seems like a strange endorsement for a gun range (the movie ends in a volcanic bloodbath), until you read the caption: the scene pictured was filmed right here at Westside. The regulars are a relaxed lot: one part is predictably made up of security and law enforcement, but the rest is a mix. "I get teachers, doctors, lawyers," says Johnson, the manager. "I get people in the public school system. I get men, women …" He says he came in years ago for a hunting license, and fell under a spell. "For me it's more of a Zen thing, being able to reach out"—aiming an invisible pistol—"and touch something at a distance."

You can do this, too. If you've gone through the first-timer application process (easy, but don't bother if you're a felon), within minutes of walking into the place you'll be holding your own .22 target rifle and listening to the expert instruction of "Tiny" John, who looks like he could shot-put a refrigerator. John's speaking style is interesting: a veneer of quick and funny on a base of no-nonsense. He's there to help you learn, but his main job is keeping you safe. He's also eerily skilled with guns. When one student worries that his rifle shoots consistently high and to the left, John silently takes it, strings an inch-wide strip of cardboard out about 30 feet, and makes a pretty line of holes right up the middle. "Seems OK," he shrugs.

CENTER FOR BOOK ARTS

28 West 27th Street, 3rd Floor
• www.centerforbookarts.org
• 212.481.0295
• Class prices vary; check website
• Transport: 1, F, M, N, R and 6 trains/23 and 28 St

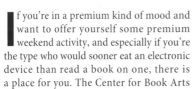

Every aspect of book making

I f you're in a premium kind of mood and want to offer yourself some premium weekend activity, and especially if you're the type who would sooner eat an electronic device than read a book on one, there is a place for you. The Center for Book Arts teaches every aspect of civilization's greatest technology, from type and ink to folding and binding, and from ancient tricks to art experiments that test what "book" really means.

Expect interesting company. "We have visual artists, designers, writers, calligraphers," says Programs Manager Sarah Nicholls. "We get a huge range of people." Nicholls speaks with friendly confidence: you may or may not know yet that you're standing in the NASA of the craft. Among one recent group of less than a dozen students there were attendees from New Haven, Washington D.C., Cuba, Japan, Argentina and Brazil. These are committed people; in any given class, some will be experts in another, complementary area.

The classes generally span a weekend. The variety of instruction brings home an overlooked fact: the simplicity of books is deceptive. "Sheet paper,

glue, thread, cloth," lists a teacher of an 18th-century German binding technique: "but all the materials affect each other." And the warmth of books is generally wrought on iron. The machines have a weighty poise and character: large machines, old-fangled machines. Some are simple, like a screw press; others are sculptures of whirring gears and rollers. There are yards of scarred drawers filled with metal type, and the wood floors are stained with inks and dyes. It's a straightforward environment, a support system for the beautiful objects made here. Letterpress, woodcut, typesetting, cut cover and stitch, leather techniques, copperplate calligraphy, illuminated manuscript … Whatever area piques your imagination, there will be someone who can show you the tricks.

COFFEE CUPPING

❸

Blue Bottle Coffee
160 Berry Street, Brooklyn
• www.bluebottlecoffee.com/cafes/berry-st
• 718.387.4160
• Free cuppings every Thursday at noon
• Transport: L train/Bedford Av

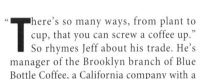

Quality control

"There's so many ways, from plant to cup, that you can screw a coffee up." So rhymes Jeff about his trade. He's manager of the Brooklyn branch of Blue Bottle Coffee, a California company with a bit of a thing about quality: many believe they roast the best coffee anywhere. Central to the process is cupping, a control that takes place at various points in the trajectory from harvested bean to the finely balanced potion you'll be content to lay down a few dollars for. Once a week the shop invites the public to experience cupping directly. If you like your coffee cheap and milky, this may not be your thing; if you're obsessed, or appreciate the lengths that obsessives will go to, don't miss it.

"Coffee is as cool as wine, for me," says Jasper Berg, Blue Bottle's wholesale trainer and leader of today's group. Berg will wreck your notion of the aggravating expert: clear-eyed, long haired, ill-shaven, and with a tattoo on either forearm, he's also smart, enthusiastic, and about as snobby as a Muppet. For half an hour he shepherds you through cupping's four stages: dry smell, where the roasted beans are coarsely ground and shaken in a bowl to release aromatic gases; wet smell, when steaming hot water is added; the break, where the surface particulate ("we call it the scum") is raked off; and finally a tasting, where a spoonful of the coffee isn't drunk so much as atomized over the palate with a blasting slurp. This isn't just a gourmand's foolery: half of the reason behind cupping is to find what might be amiss— an overdone roast or a bean with "potato defect" (a hint of stale french fry).

You'll soon understand that coffee is more complex than you thought. Some growers keep their bushes in the shade of particular trees—apple, for example—to imbue the bean with the most gossamer subtleties. Throughout,

you can see Berg weighing his perceptions: cupping is a job, and when you take part you're behind the scenes. Sampling the world's different growing regions has its own appeal. "It's not every day that you get a chance to just *taste* different places," says Berg. "Here you have an Indonesian, a Middle African, and an Ethiopian all laid out on the same table."

GAGA PEOPLE

Classes offered at various locations, usually in Brooklyn
• Check website for schedule: www.gagapeople.com
• Admission: around $15

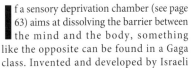

Connect to pleasure

If a sensory deprivation chamber (see page 63) aims at dissolving the barrier between the mind and the body, something like the opposite can be found in a Gaga class. Invented and developed by Israeli choreographer Ohad Naharin, Gaga is a system of movement that awakens, to a degree that newcomers might find pleasantly startling, an awareness of the flesh you travel around in. Refined at Naharin's Tel Aviv company Batsheva (declared a national treasure by Israel), Gaga technique is used as a tool by professional dancers of both contemporary and classical ballet. Anyone who has taken a class with the master himself can do an impression of Naharin's slow, sensuous instruction: "Connect to pleasurrre." It's not a connection exclusive to dancers: if you're a human animal, you have this in you already.

The method: take a standard ballet class, where the body is treated like a machine that runs a series of rigid commands, and blow it to smithereens. "Now we are going to start moving," begins today's instructor, Navarra Novy-Williams, "and for an hour, we're not going to stop." Constant motion is key. So is a heightened sensory awareness: for this reason mirrors are forbidden (Naharin: "Break your mirrors in all studios. They spoil the soul."). The vocabulary is evocative and odd: your joints are "greasy," your arms are "hungry" for space, your head "hangs on a thumb pressed to the roof of your mouth." You imagine your muscles as atoms, as mush, as a glowing color field. It starts at the top of the head, and, like an enlivening vine, grows everywhere while the pace heats up and the gestures, at first slow and small, quicken and expand. Your body grooves and explodes by turns.

By the end, you're freely improvising. Is it good dance? Maybe, maybe not—generating movement is only a part of it. One of Gaga's best tricks is guiding you toward a perception of yourself as a different sort of creature, while at the same time the normal rules of matter itself have shifted. Gravity is variable, air consistency is variable, time is variable. At certain moments—as when you writhe on the floor like a snake—an outsider peeking in the window would naturally conclude that the class has been sprayed with a few gallons of LSD. But you need to dial through some static to get in tune.

DROP-IN DRAWING AT THE MET

Metropolitan Museum of Art
1000 Fifth Avenue
• www.metmuseum.org/events/family-programs/drop-in-drawing
• 212.535.7710
• Drop-In Drawing currently held at 6:30 pm every other Friday; check website for schedule
• Transport: 6 train/77 St; 4 and 5 trains/86 St/B and C trains/81 St (walk through Central Park)

I f you've ever fixated on this or that bewitching detail of a fine painting and marveled at the craft of it, or even felt—a natural follow-up—the itch to explore that effect with your own hand, the Met has a program for you. Drop-In Drawing takes

Another kind of engagement with an object

place twice a month, and is designed to alleviate whatever art anxieties you may have built up since you were a child and could draw anything. A folding stool is provided. A drawing board too, and pencils, erasers, different tones of quality paper, all laid out in a gallery of one of the world's best collections of inspiration. You really have no excuse.

It all unfolds late during opening hours, and part of the appeal is occupying this revered space for a purpose other than stroking your chin. "It's usually some corner of the museum that nobody ever goes to," says Max, a regular. "And it's a magical place to be at night." The sessions each explore a specific area of drawing. During a focus on portraiture, you might learn from the staff that an imaginary line sweeping from the corners of your eyes and around your head will hit the tops of your ears (and one under your nose will hit the bottoms). Or that a head can be constructed as a system of two intersecting ovals: one for the outline of the face, and another for the extension of the skull back in space. But much of what you'll gain is in the area of the ineffable. "Drawing opens up another kind of engagement with an object," says Jessica Houston, a longtime instructor at the museum. "And I think in particular it kind of collapses time. Because you stand in the very same place that the artist stood when he or she made that work. It was a live thing. It was an activity. The painting is a trace of that."

You'll find that when you try to closely follow a master's steps, the work becomes more mysterious, not less. In Manet's *Boating* (1874), a man steers a sailboat, nothing behind him but calm blue waves. But the figure contains ten thousand nuances. The patch of brightness at his throat has a sheen of sweat in it. And under his brows instead of shadow there is light, and not just any light: it's the active, watery kind of sunlight reflecting from the sea. The exercise triggers a feeling that is deeper than admiration: it's a sensual bridge across time.

RARE CHEESES AT MURRAY'S

254 Bleecker Street
- www.murrayscheese.com/classes.html
- 212.243.3289
- Check website for class schedule
- Fee: varies from $40 to $120
- Transport: A, B, C, D, E, F and M trains/West 4 St; 1 train/Christopher St

> *Discover taste, discover yourself*

For over sixty years, Murray's has been supplying New York's finicky gourmands with the best cheese in the world. The place has practically symbolized the cheese-making art in its layout: down under Bleecker Street they've dug out caves where the musty and arcane process of aging takes place; on street level, there are the bright shop and cheese bar where the consumer can buy and try the wares; upstairs the air gets thinner: here the finer points are discussed in regular tastings and classes.

The strangest of these is "Rare and Unusual Cheeses." You can't appreciate what's rare without understanding what's common, so the class contains a general overview of process as well as a gentle message about appreciation. "If I'm doing my job right," says head cheesemonger Anuradha Jayakrishnan, "people have a better understanding of how to approach a cheese culture. They're blown away by how much effort and detail goes into it." Take Isle of Mull cheddar, made from the milk of cows that are fed fermented grain from a nearby whiskey distillery, or a Salers cheese from central France where the dairy cows are only milked in the presence of their newborn calves. Torta del Casar from Spain is sheep's milk curdled with thistle, a trick that goes back some two thousand years. Blue cheese is injected with mold; take a cheddar and put it through the same process and you get Dunbarton Blue, a Wisconsin variety that class leader Elizabeth Chubbuck calls "the jazz of cheese—so American."

With a half-dozen wedges on your slate that cover the gamut of pungency, and water and wine on hand, attendees are invited to analyze taste itself. The vocabulary tries to seize transient impressions: a texture is like velvet, cake, pudding; a flavor is citrusy, grassy, vegetal. One cheese comes on like charred onion. Another has a ghost of vinegar in it. The blue-cheddar hybrid has a caramel zip that suggests Crackerjack. The higher you get in fine cheese, the more room there is for subjectivity. In the end you taste to discover yourself. "I think when people are taught how," says Chubbuck, "it opens up an entirely new world of experience, an entirely new way to relate with what they're eating." Consider Bleu du Bocage, a blue cheese made—oddly, you'll learn— from goat's milk. The flavor is angry, barny, with a bitter hint of grapefruit pith and a finish that's somewhere between epoxy resin and napalm. Not your thing? Make a note.

PROLINE ARCHERY ❼

95–11 101st Avenue, Queens
• www.archeryny.com
• 718.845.9280
• Hours for instruction and non-league members vary: see website
• Two-hour introductory class, including bow rental: $20
• Transport: A train/Rockaway Blvd

> **This is where it starts**

What can a modern person do with archery skills? Take down a bear, for one. If the world's largest land predator is too much, try a deer. Or a turkey. Or a fish (really). "I could go hunting with my kids when I grow up," says Danny McGrath, a dazzle-eyed 8-year-old who has come to Proline Archery in Queens with his parents to buy his first bow. "I could be in the Olympics. I could be a lot of stuff."

Or you might just spend your time, as an entire community of focused people do, thwocking arrow after arrow into a paper target. Archery is a world, and if you're not of it already, beware: it can take over. "Once you get familiar, when you walk in the door—you get the smell," says Jack, a man with a bald head, a hero's torso, and—fittingly somehow among the quivers and the arrows—a pleated khaki kilt. He inflates his enormous chest with the ineffable aroma of archery. "And that's it," he says. "You think: this is where it starts." When Jack isn't target practicing, he's on the line helping a beginner: there's a decidedly close, even familial atmosphere here. "What you receive, you give back," he shrugs.

The range has a business end, a counter under an array of hanging bows. Which kind you prefer is a metric of personality. "I like the recurve for its style," says Ed Cortez, a Queens native and relative beginner. The recurves are the simplest sort, the weapon you'd see in the hands of an elf. "But then I look at this"—hefting a black contraption that splits the difference between a spider and a bicycle—"and I think: that looks deadly." You can also buy scent blockers to foil your prey in the woods, or any of dozens of DVDs with odder-than-average titles (*Monster Bucks*, vol. 19). There are other places that sell this stuff; here's where you should get it. "The gentlemen that own this," says Jack, "have regular jobs. They're not here to lead you the wrong way."

One of the gentlemen is Olympic archer Guy Gerig, who, after tossing the remains of his Chinese takeout, wipes his mouth, steps from behind the counter and calmly shoots three bull's-eyes at 60 feet. One of the arrows, with dead center already crowded, rips through the back of another. "It happens," Gerig acknowledges, fishing into his pocket for a replacement part from a plastic baggie full of them. Your first lesson won't cover this (it's called "Robin-Hooding"), but in two hours you'll get the basics.

SURVIVAL IN CENTRAL PARK

Mountain Scout Survival School
• www.mtnscoutsurvival.com
• Fee: $100
• Survival 1 class held in Central Park; check website for schedule
• Transport: B and C trains/103 St

Bugging out

"**A**re you gonna stay, or are you gonna bug out?" This is the question Shane Hobel will ask as you sit under a shade tree in Central Park, lulled by the background murmur of a metropolis in harmony. Hobel is the founding instructor of Mountain Scout Survival School; he has twenty years of experience helping law enforcement, military, and the private sector acquire the know-how that will become vital when the harmony goes suddenly haywire. "Bug out" is a term you'll hear a lot during the course: it means a breathless escape from a city that, due to whatever calamity, has become a trap filled with panicking idiots.

The course lasts a full day, and is the urban counterpart to a more woodsy version that Hobel offers at his training facility upstate. During the instruction these northern forests beckon like a sparkling oasis: the destroyed city is an obstacle course—of traffic, collapsed buildings, chemicals, radioactivity—that must be negotiated to get to the mainland, and further into a brave new life of roast squirrel and spring water. Central Park's North Wood serves as fill-in for the wild: there you'll make an emergency lean-to and get an overview of the principles of securing the four rock-bottom necessities: shelter, water, food, and fire. It's little more than a hint of ancient skills that your domestic kind has lost. Peculiar to the class are the techniques that might make the difference between bugging out successfully and getting crushed with the rest of the jerks. Hobel recommends learning lock-picking and how to access a building's water reservoir. "It's your environment," he says.

The style of instruction is totally unique: you might easily call Hobel paranoid, but paranoia is hindsight's preparedness. He can be rough, even browbeating ("You think I'm being harsh? You've got it *easy*"), but has a spiritual bent, hinted at by unglossed mentions of "the Elders" and shady tips like putting mugwort frond in your shoe to influence your dreams. He knows how to live rough, but he'll take whatever's available as long as it works: LED lights, contractor bags, mylar, GPS systems. And tampons. Hobel knows a hundred irregular uses for the regular tampon. Example: insert one into the spout of an empty water bottle with the bottom cut off; fill bottle halfway with charcoal dust; trail tampon string into second plastic bottle. Now you have water purification system. Someday you might be glad somebody told you.

SWORD CLASS NYC

- www.swordclassnyc.com
- 646.580.9532
- Fee: three classes, $65

> *Control a sword, control yourself*

" I n just about every samurai movie," says Raab Rashi by way of orientation, "there's a scene where one is forced to draw very quickly and make a cut before the other person can react. That's what our main form teaches." Founder and head instructor of Sword Class NYC, Rashi also teaches full-contact German broadsword and traditional kendo, but he's unique in offering Siljun Dobup, a technique invented by a Korean grandmaster (Rashi's personal teacher) and based on centuries-old Japanese fighting tradition.

Siljun Dobup translates as "real sword training"–a little strangely, because it draws powerfully on the imagination. Advanced students attack rice mats soaked in water and rolled around a stick of green bamboo to simulate a human limb. (Rashi: "It's actually much easier to slice through than you'd think.") If simulated dismemberment is more vivid than you want from a martial arts class, you'd best move along. Siljun Dobup is a highly decorous, even ceremonialized approach to technique, but the gestures are deadly serious. What's more, mental projection is part of it. At your first class, you'll learn to sheathe the sword with a quick sideways flick. It's one of eight or so choreographed movements in a sequence, but the purpose is to shake off your phantom opponent's arterial blood. Strict codes of beautiful movement: it's like Zen tea (see page 277), but with weapons. And, like Zen tea, the benefit is only partly what you see on the surface. "If you can control a sword," says Rashi, "then you can control yourself. And if you can control yourself, you can control the world around you." The sentiment is as old as Yoda, but it sounds fresh when you're holding a blade.

Intermediate students have steel weapons; you'll get one made of oak. At first, you won't be any good with it, and why this is will be unclear. Rashi seems to embody this mystery: not tall, not conspicuously muscled, and courteous, when he picks up the sword some hidden faculty slots into place and he becomes a Killer. "The sword rewards a relaxed approach," he says, effortlessly whistling his blade in an overhand chop. When you try, there's no sound. The instructor takes your wooden sword, chops—and it whistles. You try again: nothing. The whistle is called *tachi kaze*, "sword wind," and its lack reveals, almost cruelly, an imperfect form. If the prospect of controlling the world around you isn't incentive enough, chasing *tachi kaze* should be enough to get you to at least your second lesson.

PUPPET KITCHEN

220 East 4th Street
• www.puppetkitchen.com
• 706.478.7738
• Fee: $35 dollars for groups of five or more; other arrangements can be made
• Transport: F train/2 Av; J and M trains/Essex St

> **A workshop where you create your own**

E ric Wright confesses that when people ask what he does for a living and he says "puppeteer," if they aren't at least a little interested he secretly assumes there's something wrong with them. It's what you expect to hear from a puppeteer, but he has a point. Puppets plumb some fundamental magic. A sock is a sock until you put it on your hand—then it's alive. Where exactly this quickening process takes place is a subject you can freely explore at one of the Puppet Kitchen's workshops, where you'll take a colorful piece of shaggy fabric, some glue and thread, and create a surprisingly viable hand puppet.

"We're a one-stop-shop puppet studio," says Wright, preparing for class in the Kitchen's workroom, which was in fact once an industrial kitchen for the Lower Eastside Girls Club. Now it's full of bookcases and stacks of plastic tubs stuffed with fabric, and an entire wall of spray paints, and half-finished masks and cardboard body parts hanging from lines like laundry. The company has done extensive work for stage and screen; the classes are outreach. "We're all about expanding the art," says Wright. "People build what are commonly thought of as puppets—these little furry Muppety things—but they also see the other kinds of stuff that we get to do and the different things puppets can be."

Class begins with choosing your color among a stack of precut plush fabric (Wright: "Pick a pelt") and gluing it to a disc of corrugated black plastic which, folded on itself, will eventually be the inside of your little guy's mouth (and where you grasp with your hand). After a few minutes spent stitching up their back, the slack puppets are spread out on the table: faceless, yawning things. "This is where yours stops looking like everybody else's," Wright says, distributing scissors for haircuts and various beads and fuzzies for parts. "Be bold. A puppet—unlike a person—has a character that comes first from the way it looks." This observation is either wise or naive: you will be too distracted by the flying fur to decide. One by one the puppets emerge from a mist of anonymity and become the bizarrely alive playthings that enchant normal humans. The last minutes of class are a riot of impromptu puppet comedy. "Infusing that sense of play into how people live is so important," says a satisfied Wright. "Getting up to actively play is just … It's just great, you know?"

TANGO IN THE PARK

Around the Shakespeare statue in Central Park (at the head of the Mall at around 66th Street)
• Every Saturday, June to September, 6 – 9 pm; free lesson with a professional at 7:30 pm
• Admission: free

TANGO TONIGHT

On Saturday evenings in the warmer months, you might walk down the aisle of stately elms in the Mall and detect thin, seductive strains of music, like old radio. Follow and you'll arrive at what appears to be a collection of ghosts floating around the statue of Shakespeare. It's a serious business: the expressions on their faces are contented but curiously vacant. Tango has hypnotized them.

"Everyone here is a professional," says a tanned man in a dress shirt and a red vest, "just like in jail, everyone is innocent." This is Igor: he's suave, even Montalbanesque, and a few years into his second handsomeness; his slight accent makes everything he says sound like an exotic life lesson. He has no partner—yet. "Some of these women, if they don't recognize you, they will not dance." Looking out, you can see why: the ladies, in general, sway with their eyes closed, a controlled swoon, as they glide in a tight embrace with their expert partner. It takes more than a degree of trust. "But I will dance with anybody," he says, his smile suggesting a generally omnivorous policy toward women. Along the metal rail are onlookers: mostly tourists and the curious. Igor scans the possibilities, operating on the principle that every female is secretly burning to surrender to the transports of tango. He may be right. One lady catches his eye. She wears a silk dress and high heels, and stands smoothing a shawl over her shoulders in a pool of lamplight—which, with the built-in nostalgia of the music, may be the surest way to make yourself romantically interesting. "OK," Igor says, "I go find my victim …" And he slips into the mobile throng. A few moments later he and the woman are locked in a sway, foreheads pressed together.

If this game seems out of your league, local tango teachers set up a few feet away, where they offer free lessons to left-footed novices. You'll need a partner, and the assigned roles are the very fabric of the dance: somebody leads, somebody's led. It's part of tango's sexual radiation, but it also keeps the crowd in order: tango couples glide, and curve, and maneuver in unexpected patterns. Nobody talks: nobody makes any noise at all. When 9 o'clock comes around, the speaker is switched off, the music is packed up, and the ghosts collect their coats and bags from around the base of the statue and disperse. All that's left is a message in chalk on the stone paving: TANGO TONIGHT.

CENTER FOR ALTERNATIVE PHOTOGRAPHY ⑫

36 East 30th Street
- www.capworkshops.org
- 917.288.0343
- See website for class schedule
- Office hours: Monday to Friday 10 am – 6 pm
- Transport: 6, N and R trains/28 St

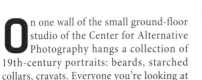

Vividly chemical

On one wall of the small ground-floor studio of the Center for Alternative Photography hangs a collection of 19th-century portraits: beards, starched collars, cravats. Everyone you're looking at has moved on, metaphysically, but their hard stares remain. Now imagine the casual historian of the year 2143 gazing interestedly at you, by means of … what? Instagram page? iPhoto album? Selfie tweet? Today's digital orgy makes images cheap. If you find something wanting there, or if you love it all but are curious about the slow, thoughtful processes of yore, C.A.P. is the place.

"The digital age is a flattening process," says executive director Geoffrey Berliner, probably not for the first time. Berliner has two days' worth of stubble and the pleasantly jagged talking style of a guy whose brain whirrs slightly faster than a single mouth can deal with. His basement is full of antiquated equipment of glass and brass, and his attitudes are perfectly expressed by the camera he carries in his pocket: a digital point-and-shoot outfitted with an antique lens. Modernity is well and good. "But there are some people," he says, "that like the slower approach of alternate processes, people with a particular voice that don't necessarily fit in. It's not a matter of better or worse, but that everybody has something that fits well." What fits you might be one of the many forms the C.A.P. offers in hands-on classes: platinum printing, glass negative, daguerreotype, cyanotype … Vividly chemical processes that speak to the very origins of photography, and require some finesse.

For a taste of wet-plate collodion photography ("the Polaroid of the 19th century"), get your portrait made in the Tintype Studio. You can even watch as the process unfolds. First, a plate is coated in a syrup of metal salts and ether, then soaked in silver nitrate and loaded into a wooden frame. This sensitized surface is a one-of-a-kind, a positive: after absorbing your immortal image as you sit on a stool and stare into a lens the size of a tea saucer, the plate is taken back to the dark room and developed in chemical baths, where it becomes the photo: you watch in the amber light as your unique portrait blooms into existence. "If you're interested in photography, that's great," says Berliner. "If you're not, but you want a keepsake, a *thing*, not a pixel, not something that's living in the *cloud*, then you come here for this crafted object that will last a long, long, long, long time."

> The first picture ever taken in the New World was of a church on Broadway. New York has been a photography town ever since.

KNIFE SKILLS CLASS AT BROOKLYN KITCHEN ⑬

100 Frost Street, Brooklyn and 600 Eleventh Avenue, Manhattan
• 718.389.2982
• See website for class schedule:
www.thebrooklynkitchen.com/about-brooklyn-kitchen/classes/
• Class fee: $65
• Transport: L train/Lorimer St

Where serious cooking begins

Everything about fine cuisine that might cause anxiety—the precision, the traditionalism, the prickliness that comes with refinement—can be located in the knife. Knives are *already* forbidding, and when you see someone who has mastered the chef's moves, who can take a stack of vegetables and *shoonk shoonk shoonk* it into a pile of tiny cubes and slivers, without any fingertips in it, you can be sure that you're in the presence of cooking comfort in general. The Brooklyn Kitchen in Williamsburg has a whole roster of classes; it's no mystery that basic knife skills is a prerequisite for all of them. This is where getting serious about preparing food begins.

First the guiding principles. There's a reason for cutting food up into dainty shapes before cooking instead of, say, smashing with a hammer. First, discipline breeds safety, and a gore-free kitchen is a happy one. Second, standard shapes are practical. "It will cook at the same rate," says instructor Kate Duff, "and have the same flavor profile." That cheerful Duff takes for granted that "flavor profile" is among your chief concerns already makes you feel better about yourself. Third, precisely chopped food simply looks nice, and food that looks nice is food you're more likely to enjoy putting in your mouth.

After learning the parts of a standard chef's knife—spine, bolster, tang—and the correct way to whip up the edge with a honing steel, Duff shows the gesture that will take you as far down the path to mastery as you wish to go: with the point always in contact with the cutting board, glide the blade forward as if on a rail until it's flat on the cutting surface; then lift and move it back again. Do this confidently and there's a circular, machinelike beauty. You dice the air for a while to practice, and then Duff leads you through a host of vegetables, fed into the eager blade by a protective hand position she calls the "angry bear claw." Class wraps up with a magically clever method for cutting a large onion.

Duff, whose own knife is a Japanese marvel of folded steel, doesn't glamour up the tool, and—more to her credit—doesn't try to sell you one. "You don't need a million knives," she says, quickly reducing a handful of parsley sprigs to green dust. "And you don't need to spend a lot. But somewhere out there, there's the knife for you."

HISTORY

CONFERENCE HOUSE

298 Satterlee Street, Staten Island
• www.conferencehouse.org
• 718.984.6046
• The house can be visited April to December; the reenactment takes place every year on September 11
• Transport: S59 or S78 bus/Hylan Blvd – Craig Av; Staten Island Railway train/Tottenville (last stop)

King or country?

On a hill overlooking the southern tip of Staten Island stands the city's oldest manor, the Conference House, which hosts a curious ritual. Every year in mid-September reenactors gather in their buckle shoes and bonnets to recreate an episode in local history when the fate of America was decided during the course of a single lunch.

We're in September of 1776. Under the shade trees there is an elegant table: British commander Howe—or the actor who wears his wig and breeches—has invited Benjamin Franklin, John Adams and Edward Rutledge from the Continental Congress to discuss an immediate end to the Revolutionary War. You might get swept up in the play. "Are you ready," asks a man in full military kit, "to fight for king and country?" He has a contemporary glint in his eye, but other reenactors maintain a glassy earnestness: "I am but a poor farmer," says an elderly man in the green coat of a Loyalist; he sided with the British, he claims, because he can't stand the thought of more violence after the gruesome Battle of Brooklyn two weeks ago. When asked how he thinks the historic meeting will turn out, the man wobbles and blinks. "I would not hazard a guess," he says, and then nibbles some hardtack from a Ziploc baggie.

Reenactment is more often miss than hit; the Conference House does it right. Smiling women stir iron pots of apples and bacon over smoky flame, wiping tears from their eyes on the hems of their aprons. There are butter-churners and quilt-makers and men firing muskets at the sky. The air is filled with dulcimer music and the tang of burnt wood. At the appointed hour a fife and drum trill from the direction of the beach: the Yanks have arrived, as they do every year, in a rowboat from New Jersey. After trooping from the landing and up the hill, the proud rebels seat themselves uneasily around the table ("The menu," says a young lady reading over a loudspeaker, "included good claret, tongue, ham, and mutton"). Commander Howe makes civilized and condescending overtures of compromise which foxy Ben Franklin rejects on principle, while John Adams appears to fight an urge to vomit. "And so the Americans," the young lady announces, "resisted the temptation to compromise their ideals of liberty." The drum rattles, the fife tweets, and the delegates head back to their rowboat, trailed by whooping kids.

TRACKING MINETTA BROOK

Around Washington Square Park
• Steve Duncan's site: www.undercity.org
• Transport: A, B, C, D, E, F and M trains/W 4 St; N and R trains/8 St – NYU

One of the most suggestive, eerie, and seemingly fictitious features of the Village is Minetta Brook, a river that flows secretly underground. There are tales of flooded restaurants, and men with fishing poles gathered around holes in the concrete

> *An underground river flows through the Village*

floors of basements, and garden fountains tapping the black water deep below. But Minetta exists. It was once a creek full of trout; sometime in the early 1800s it got entombed by a blanket of humming metropolis.

Today you can follow the course of the buried stream as it flows from about Fifth Avenue and out to the Hudson River. With an ordinary flashlight you can even see it, but you'll need the tour plan of Steve Duncan, Internet personage and expert on all things subterranean. "From the tops of bridges to the depths of sewer tunnels," according to Duncan, "these explorations of the urban environment help me puzzle together the interconnected, multidimensional history and complexity of the great metropolises of the world." The hidden stream is the subject of his doctoral thesis. It's also very clearly his obsession: when he talks about it—gesturing with scuffed hands, a rolled cigarette wagging from his lip—you know you've found an authority. Here are the highlights of his recent tour of the Village's own hidden river.

45 WEST 12TH STREET

This house is a relic of the old stream course. It overlaps its neighbor oddly, and actually has a wedge-shaped floor plan. The creek used to cut a diagonal across the lot, and the structure was built to skirt it.

60 9TH STREET

The address doesn't interest us: what does is the manhole cover in the street out front. It's a DPW (Department of Public Works) type, with large holes. Look in one hole and shine a flashlight down another. The water you see, according to Duncan, is a combination of "natural water flow and water used by residents in the area." Minetta, in other words, has been channeled into the city's infrastructure.

MINETTA STREET

Here, as the name indicates, is deep in Brook territory. The kinked shape of this street (unique in Manhattan) is said to follow the path of the old water. If you hunt out the manhole cover—a DPW "hexagon" model like the one above—you'll see a steady flow, and be as close to the original stream as you can get without a crowbar and hip waders.

VERTICAL TOUR

Cathedral Church of St. John the Divine
Amsterdam Avenue and 112th Street
• Check website for tour schedule: www.stjohndivine.org
• 212.316.7490
• Transport: 1 train/110 St – Cathedral Pkwy

Medieval Manhattan

The Cathedral of St. John the Divine, New York City's own pile of Romanesque, is the most massive cathedral in the world. Begun in 1892, it's still unfinished today. To understand how this could be, look to another church towering a few blocks away in the northwest: Riverside, the nation's tallest, likewise inspired by medieval French architecture. Riverside broke ground in 1927, and was finished just three years later. The difference is, when you ascend that building, you take an elevator: the ornate stone is a shell hung on a skyscraper's skeleton of I-beams and rivets. St. John the Divine is stone on stone all the way through. This cathedral's parts were carved whole from the earth, and there are few tricks here that would surprise a mason from the Middle Ages. You can appreciate this fact to its fullest on one of the regular Vertical Tours, where you scale a stair up through the cathedral's walls.

The tour is a lesson in the building's history, and a review of the art historical symbols frozen in its stone and glass, which you'll see from a dizzying vantage in the upper-level clerestory. (Don't miss the depiction of the invention of television in the stained glass bay devoted to the history of communication: these weird collisions of ancient and modern are New York to the core.) Peering out, roughly halfway up the nave's 124-foot height, the church seems even vaster: you're skating a cliff edge between a canyon and a vault. On either side stretches an interior longer than two football fields end to end.

But the best part of the Vertical Tour is getting into the building's stone skin: it's a fun that has a touch of the devious as you scrape through spiral stairs and duck under the shoulders of buttresses. And after you've passed up and over the echoing nave and into the uppermost hollow—a vast network of support beams called the *forêt* (forest)—you'll be taking in a site that, architecturally speaking, you have no business accessing. It's the cathedral's crazy attic. And probably the only place in the city where you can see the regular range of tiled hills that form the *other* side of a major vaulted ceiling.

MOVIES AT THE NEW-YORK HISTORICAL SOCIETY

⑰

170 Central Park West
• www.nyhistory.org
• 212.873.3400
• Check website for film schedule
• Admission: $20
• Transport: B and C trains/81 St; 1 train/79 St

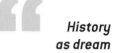

History as dream

The New-York Historical Society isn't exactly entertainment: you pass through that marble Greek portico into a house of learning. In the main hall are the pistols used in the Burr-Hamilton duel, and Indian artifacts, and fragments of the doomed lead statue of King George III that once stood in Bowling Green. In the library you contemplate manuscripts and maps. But since the 2012 restoration, the Society also hosts various lectures and viewings in a comfortable balconied theater. Here, during winter and spring, you can get your history as dream, in the form of classic movies.

"It gives people a chance to finally see the great classic movies in a theater," says program director Dale Gregory. "But it's not just the films, it's the guest speakers who come. They're all fascinating, wonderful." Each film is introduced by an academic or professional of tested eminence: before you see *Young Mr. Lincoln*, you hear about it from Lincoln scholar and biographer Harold Holzer. *I Know Where I'm Going* is set up by decorated editor Thelma Schoonmaker, whose late husband directed. You've probably caught *The Third Man* at some point in your life, but not framed by *New Yorker* film critic lion David Denby.

When the audience has settled in, Denby sets up the play of bitterness and moral blur in the 1949 film. "We are in Vienna, three and a half years after the war is over. And I think we can say the grownups have taken over." Good of Denby to attune you to the themes extracted over many viewings, but he has room also for the enlivening anecdote: Graham Greene, who wrote the original treatment, believed for example that American innocence was a danger to the world, "that it should be like a leper carrying a little bell, warning people." Denby's partner on the dais, journalist Kati Marton, points out the gem of a detail that even the children in *The Third Man* are rotten: it features "probably the only sinister 6-year-old in movies."

The presenters get something out of the arrangement, too. "I like talking," says Denby. "Not giving lectures, but talking informally with someone you like that you can play off of." Major themes are aligned beforehand, but the conversation is loose: a couple of friendly experts who happen to share a room with you for a few minutes before the house lights dip, and the flickering screen becomes a window onto the past.

TWEED COURTHOUSE TOUR

52 Chambers Street
• Check website for schedule and to reserve a spot:
www.nyc.gov/html/artcom/html/tours/tweed.shtml
• Or call: 212.788.2656
• Transport: 1, 2, 3, A, C and J trains/Chambers St; 2 and 3 trains/Park Pl;
N and R trains/City Hall; 4, 5 and 6 trains/Brooklyn Bridge

> *The house
> that graft built*

There are good enough architectural reasons to visit the Tweed Courthouse. Fully renovated as the headquarters of the Department of Education, the old building shocked workers when the decades of cheap paint were peeled off to reveal vividly colored brickwork—the best example of the style in the city. The place had slowly slumped into rot during the 1970s. People found the courthouse almost morally repellent: it had been built a century earlier to be the city's main seat of justice, but the builder—and namesake—was the biggest crook in American history. William "Boss" Tweed and his ring of cronies had absolute rule in the 1860s and 70s, skimming hundreds of millions of dollars by inflating the costs of the courthouse construction. The final price was double what was paid for the entire state of Alaska. This is the other, stranger reason for visiting: the whole building is a monument to corruption.

Tweed contained more personality than seems to be available currently. "He was over 6 feet tall," says guide Patricia Orfanos, "300 pounds. He walked these streets and the people who came here, particularly the Irish, knocked on his door for jobs and housing. He asked only one thing in return. Votes." The massive tensions of the period are embedded in the architecture; this building, constructed during the Civil War, is at war with itself. Two different designers with very different ideas went at it over the course of twenty years, and the result is one of the city's oddest mixes: classical cast iron and medieval brick. Throughout construction, money flowed into Tweed's pockets—but not directly. "One person paid off another," says Orfanos, "who paid off another, who paid off another. They really didn't understand the scheme even when it was printed in the paper."

One man who got it, and hounded Boss Tweed through his political cartoons (fat Tweed with a bag of money in place of a head, or staring with cold reptilian eyes), was the brilliant artist Thomas Nast. When the politician was finally nabbed, justice resumed a proper footing: he was convicted in the crooked courthouse he had built. And in the end Nast was delivered a fantastic bonus when Tweed, after escaping to Spain, was caught again because he was recognized from the printed cartoons.

FOLLOW THE CROTON TRAIL

The Bronx portion of the trail starts at the top of Van Cortlandt Park, where Hancock Avenue meets Forest Avenue (Yonkers) and descends to High Bridge at the Harlem River (at 170th Street)

New York, lost civilization

I n the late 1830s, New York took on its greatest public works project: connecting Manhattan, which suffered from a scarcity of fresh water and from all that goes with it (disease, fire hazard, drunkenness), to the sprawling Croton River 40 miles to the north. The path of the original Croton Aqueduct is dotted by remnants: gatehouses, paths, towers, and Gotham's oldest bridge. Follow them and you'll get as close as you can in the city to discovering ancient ruins.

The strangest piece of aqueduct infrastructure is also the most remote: the stone weir in Van Cortlandt Park in the Bronx. A weir is a station of flow control: here water could spill off, fresh air could waft in, and the underground tunnels could be accessed. This one is special because you come to it in the middle of a nature trail, like a sun-worshipper's temple suddenly appearing in the jungle. The stone is old enough to be well-crumbled in places; an elm tree grows right out of the roof, and even the graffiti has the jumbled charm of a forgotten alphabet. If you've got an eager imagination, you'll sense the specter of History pacing around; if not, there's a city slicker's fill of trees and birds. Dedicated aqueduct fans will, of course, swoon.

The Van Cortlandt Park website advises that the Croton Aqueduct trail is "cut by Major Deegan Freeway," which is like saying that the way to England is cut by the Atlantic. In fact, for explorers of these parts, the ramps of whooshing traffic are the primary bummer. The best place to pick up the trail again is probably Aqueduct Avenue, which starts at Kingsbridge Road and makes a pretty straight shot (the Parks Department calls it "Aqueduct Walk") to East Burnside Avenue, where there's a prominent stone gatehouse. The Bronx portion of the trail ends at the Harlem River at Sedgwick Avenue and 170th Street: put your feet there and it will be plain enough why. There stretches the oldest bridge in the city, High Bridge, built specifically for this massive works project, to deliver fresh water from the mainland to a parched Manhattan.

CHURCH OF ST. MARY THE VIRGIN

145 West 46th Street
- www.stmvirgin.org
- 212.869.5830
- Transport: N, Q, R, 7 and S trains/Times Sq

Impossible in Times Square

A t some point you're going to find yourself in Times Square. It's inevitable. Before despairing at its unholy blend of human chaos, visual bullying, and the corporate leer (or enjoying it: see page 153), hop down 46th Street to the most surprising church in the city. Later, when you show the place to friends, amazement is nearly guaranteed. St. Mary the Virgin is a 19th-century Gothic church that, while handsome on the outside, is unbelievable within. How this dark cavern of architecture, lanced with amber light through the stained glass, can fit in the middle of the block is a riddle. "You got Rockefeller on one side," says Stefan, the custodian, "and you got Times Square on another, and all the theater around us. When they walk by here they go, 'Huh?'" aping a dumbfounded local. "Everybody's just amazed that there's this gem in the middle of everything."

For the full effect, enter from 47th Street, where the back door is just a limestone surround in a wall of yellow brick. Around you are a coffee shop, 24-hour parking, a diner, a Mediterranean restaurant, and the dull Mordor of the looming News Corporation headquarters building on Sixth Avenue. From the sidewalk you can feel the darkened church's currents of cool air and incense. Duck through the door, and within a dozen paces you're in front of a great pillar at the apse. If you marvel at how the tall nave can fit in here, continue on to the side chapels where the church pushes out further, and then further still to a degree that screws with most of what you know about physics.

There's an added attraction here. The building is, aside from surprising, also a pioneer (and a true New Yorker): St. Mary the Virgin is the first steel-frame church in the world. With luck, you might get a tour of the basement with friendly archivist Dick Leitsch. "They'd never built a church like this before, so they didn't know what kind of bracing they needed. Totally overkill," he chuckles, flipping a light switch to reveal a maze of supporting steel trusses. "No way this is ever going to fall down."

BROOKLYN ARMY TERMINAL TOUR

140 58th Street, Brooklyn
• www.bklynarmyterminal.com
• Tours offered by Turnstile Tours: www.turnstiletours.com
• 347.903.8687
• Fee: $22
• Transport: N and R trains/59 St (Brooklyn)

A time-saving engineering marvel

In a part of Brooklyn that can be rough and unforgiving, in a facility that is generally closed to the curious, you'll find one of the true jaw-droppers among New York's structures. The Brooklyn Army Terminal is better than beautiful: it's authentically strange. The open atrium, raked by sunbeams and echoing with the flutters of pigeons, is lined with jutting balconies that cascade down the walls to a double set of rusted train tracks. The pattern followed seems at least half inspired by science fiction, but the surfaces show the scuffs, rust, and stains of nearly a century of use.

"The US enters World War I in April of 1917," says today's guide, Andrew Gustafson, "and we quickly realize that America's infrastructure is hugely inadequate to meeting that task." New York was the largest port in the country, but by November the trains were jammed from New Jersey all the way to Pittsburgh. The solution was to construct a time-saving engineering marvel: a lading system where train cargo was lifted by an overhead crane that skated under a glass ceiling, stocking multi-story warehouses by means of staggered balconies and served by a fleet of electric trollies, 100 elevators, and prodigious manpower. From storage the cargo could be moved via sky bridges to ships waiting on the waterfront, and on to the troops overseas.

There are moments on the tour when you can see all the way down these behemoths, Buildings A and B. "The designer, Cass Gilbert, was known for his skyscrapers," says Gustafson. "This is more of a landscraper." The overall length: 960 feet, more than three football fields end to end. Gilbert's jewel, the Woolworth Building (see page 177), is notable for its grandeur and European elegance; the Brooklyn Army Terminal has a form determined by the homely demands of speed and efficiency, and the visual impact contains a note of indifferent power. The crane-and-balcony lading system was borrowed from a Ford automobile factory; when expansive, single-floor manufacturing plants became the standard, most of these odd structures went to the wrecking ball. "The fact that we still have this here preserved," says Gustafson, "and add that it was designed by Cass Gilbert, makes this a really significant structure."

When the terminal was completed (it took only a year), the warehouses were the largest reinforced concrete buildings in the world.

LOEW'S JERSEY WONDER THEATRE

54 Journal Square, Jersey City, New Jersey
• www.loewsjersey.org
• 201.798.6055
• Ticket price: $?
• Transport: PATH train via either Journal Square – 33rd Street line or World Trade Center – Newark line: get off at Journal Square station. The theater is across the street.

> *The last real movie palace*

I t's the weekend before Halloween, and Loew's Jersey in Jersey City has a line of gabbing movie lovers stretching around the block. They've come to see a couple of classic fright films: *The Bride of Frankenstein* (1935) and *Phantom of the Opera* (1925). Uniquely, they've also come to see them in their original setting. Of New York's great movie palaces from the 1920s and 30s, a few survive: at once tumbledown and opulent, they hang on as crazy façades or have been restored for concerts, performing arts or church services. In only one of them can you actually still see a *movie*. This is it.

Loew's Jersey needs some investigating, and some patience. The theater has a patchy screening schedule, because nothing this marvelous can flourish under the reign of the bright, bland Cineplexes, with their nine-dollar candy and satanic policy of demanding money for a ticket and then selling your captive brain to pre-show advertisers. But there's a regular lineup for Halloween, when the delirious energy of cinema's Golden Age creeps out like a spirit, and draws the public to the old palace's sweeping stairs, marble columns and vaulted ceilings.

As the line shuffles into the lobby, every ticket holder does the same thing: cast a stunned gaze around the tall glowing interior. Loew's Jersey is special even among outrageous palaces: it's one of the so-called Wonder Theatres,

five flagship venues built by Marcus Loew in the late 20s, so named because each was equipped with a Wonder Morton organ. The one here is the restored original, making Loew's Jersey even more special for being the only Wonder Theatre with a working instrument. Early horror films have an edge here, because before they screen, the organ is raised on a mechanical spinning platform in the orchestra pit as though delivered by infernal forces. Then it is played by a master under the towering flicker of black and white on the screen, filling the old palace with a dramatic rumble that will change the way you thought about how moviegoers in the 20s enjoyed their "silent" films.

STRANGE

SENSORY DEPRIVATION

Blue Light Floatation
- www.bluelightfloatation.com
- Contact Sam Zeiger: 212.989.6061
- Basic one-hour session: $80
- Transport: 1, C, E, F and M trains/23 St

*Alone
at last*

Can you experience absolute nothingness? You can get close. First, you need perfect dark. And perfect silence. Then a bath heated to precisely 94 degrees—the temperature of human skin. Now add salt, so the bather will float in a state of ideal repose: suspended in nothing, staring at nothing, hearing nothing. Under these conditions, in the absence of all stimuli, the difference between the body and the mind fades away. It's as close as you can get to being a brain in a jar.

The technique is called floatation, or sensory deprivation, and for nearly thirty years Manhattanite Sam Zeiger has been offering it to the public. Dissolving the mind–body barrier is a tool for meditation, and this—as the Tibetan tchotchkes on his shelves and tables suggest—is how Zeiger got into it. Interestingly, sensory deprivation is also used as a form of torture. "Probably the biggest fear people have is confronting themselves," Zeiger says. "In the tank there are no distractions." Peering into that abyss can make a certain type go nuts.

Only one way to find out. Aside from the glimpse of madness, you might be put off by the setup: Blue Light Floatation is really just Zeiger's studio in Chelsea. Showering in a strange man's apartment and letting him enclose you, naked, in a black and steaming chamber to confront your deepest anxieties isn't everybody's idea of a thrill. Know that Zeiger is an attentive man with a great fund of calm, and between sessions the water is sterilized with ozone.

Once on your back in the brine and the dark, shut off from the trillion clacks and groans of Manhattan, the first sensation is an illusion of spinning. It's as though your mind, taken aback by the stillness, needs to fake a little hubbub. This is the effect many floaters seek: the brain craves input, and when it's withheld will gladly invent. In other words, you can hallucinate. You'll likely need a few sessions to get there. During an hour of void, it will take a moment just to relax; then you will have to overcome the deafening busyness of the body. You can hear not only your heartbeat, but the whooshing nuances of every thump. A tiny rising bubble clatters like a marble in a cement stairwell. A blink rustles like a beating wing. But when you let go, the black seems to open up, and then grow wider, and then yawn out to infinity.

GARBAGE MUSEUM

343 East 99th Street
• Not technically open to the public: try your luck
• Transport: 6 train/96 St

> **Why would somebody throw that away?**

That *Billy Joel's Greatest Hits* album you threw away in 1995, for a perfectly good reason, exists somewhere. It might be floating in the ocean, or under 40 feet of rot in a landfill, or ash on the wind. Or, if it's lucky, sitting in a clean crate with other undesirables in a Sanitation Department depot on East 99th Street as one of thousands of "exhibits" in the Garbage Museum.

The museum isn't in any way official, and you won't find it in any guide to the city. What it offers isn't even really intended for your amusement. It's a vast collection of objects that, for whatever reason, prompted a trash collector on his rounds to pause and ask the question: Why would somebody throw *that* away? Sanitation workers are the ultimate arbiters of value in New York City, and from time to time they grant reprieves. As powers go, this one is pretty great. Unloved toys, frumpy technology, posters in cheap frames, paintings by artists with no discernible talent, silent cuckoo clocks, second-place bowling trophies. Many of the objects fall into the flexible "perfectly good" category: old books and albums, kitchenware and sports equipment. Others are freakish riddles: a real dog, enormous, muscled, stuffed like a hunter's memento.

As with most great things, the Garbage Museum owes its existence to the quirks of one man. Nelson Molina first started bringing in objects off the street in 1981 to decorate his own area of the locker room. Slowly, the exhibit expanded as co-workers added their own rescued items. "It doesn't matter what it is," Molina told the *Times*. "As long as it's cool, I can hang it up and I've got a place for it."

What the Garbage Museum makes a place for isn't what you would choose to make a place for, and this is the better part of what's good about it. While you probably won't be chased out ("It's not for me to tell you where you can go and can't go," says one worker on the sidewalk out front), you won't be pandered to. These guys have made a display of our collective sense of value. It's about us, but not for us.

KINGS COUNTY DISTILLERY

Brooklyn Navy Yard, Building 121
- www.kingscountydistillery.com
- Admission (includes a tasting): $8
- Tours every Sunday, 2:30 – 5:30 pm
- Transport: F train/York St; A and C trains/High St

The first NYC whiskey since Prohibition

I n 2009, New York passed the Farm Distillery Law: it allows a farmer to make spirits, provided that at least half the grain used is locally grown. Oddly, the law doesn't state that the farm distiller has to actually own a farm. Brooklyn college friends Colin Spoelman and David Haskell glimpsed a bright future through this loophole: they founded Kings County Distillery, and so became the first producers of whiskey in New York City since Prohibition.

Kings County is also the only place in the city where, on any given weekend, you can watch how this is done. The distillery is located at the Navy Yards in a century-old gabled brick building. The inside makes the best of a leave-it-alone esthetic: the Corinthian columns are scaly with old paint; sunlight angles through the lancet windows onto a scarred floor and an assembly of gear that has a touch of the mad scientist—bottles and tubes, networks of copper pipe, steaming vats. The smell is totally unique, wholesome without being exactly appetizing—somewhere between mown grass and athlete's foot. It's the perfume of a time-honored chemistry: yeast devouring the sugars in grain. "Yeast loves sugar," says Jonathan Wingo, leader of today's tour. "And when it consumes it, produces two awesome things. One is alcohol." The other is CO_2: as the corn mash soaks in plastic tubs, the surface trembles with released bubbles. Wingo knows booze: he not only explains the organic nuances that distinguish and create it, but also the surprising degree to which it has modeled the nation's history.

And local history. We tend to associate whiskey with somewhere else: a forested backwater, a Scottish highland. The very word "moonshine" summons cricket and dew. But New Yorkers, particularly with the Irish arrival in the mid-1800s, have always made it. To their credit, the guys here won't sing you a romantic song about a local ghost slipping into the bottle. "It's not a distillery by the ocean that gets battered by the sea spray," laughs Spoelman. "Whiskey is actually much more of an industrial product than an agricultural one. It's huge amounts of chemicals. But I do think place and time hold a psychological significance, if not a taste significance. And to my mind, that is actually what whiskey is about: not exclusively what it tastes like but what it means and represents."

MUSEUM

Cortlandt Alley between Franklin and White Streets
• www.mmuseumm.com
• Admission: free
• Open Saturday and Sunday 11 am – 7 pm
• Transport: N, Q, R, J and 6 trains/Canal St

> *Exhibits in an abandoned freight elevator*

Museum is an exhibition space, little more than 5 feet square, that occupies an abandoned freight elevator shaft in a downtown Manhattan alley. You can only enter on the weekend, but the steel doors come equipped with viewing ports and a number to call to learn about the odd objects that line the walls (all visible at once), making it the only 24-hour museum in the city.

"Welcome," says Alex Kalman, springing the padlock on the doors and sweeping his arm with self-mocking grandeur. The first thing to say about the tiny space is: it walks a narrow line of what constitutes "museummness." Trim design, white molding, rich velvet, etched brass plaques. There's even a "café" (a narrow electric espresso machine) and a "gift shop" (a foot-wide shelf with pencils printed with the tasteful Museum logo). Because the trappings are so finely observed, it's a challenge to figure out whether you're in a parody or not. Kalman comes clean: "We're absolutely playing with the idea of a museum," he says. But it's thoughtful play. Kalman founded the space with his business partners and friends since high school as another outlet for the ideas the trio explores at Red Bucket Films (the offices are around the corner on Broadway). "We're saying: Why can't we call *this* a museum? But at the same time trying to really respect the key ingredients."

All of this falls apart if the exhibits fail to intrigue, and that you'll decide for yourself. But expect objects with built-in riddles. Why is that plain brown shoe here? It's the one hurled at George W. Bush by an Iraqi reporter in 2008. Come also to see ornate soap carvings by gifted neo-Nazi zealots with eternities of free time in prison. Or probably the only collection of Disney-themed children's bulletproof backpacks. "No art for art's sake," says Kalman, stating a cardinal rule. "These have to be artifacts, things that have kind of passed through society as part of our nature. And it's up to us to look at society through them." Kalman, curious and good-humored, has created a testing ground for what we consider worth elevating. Museum isn't a comment on what an exhibition space should be, only on what it could be if he and his buddies ran it. Which, lucky for Cortlandt Alley, they do.

DACHSHUNDS IN THE PARK

Washington Square Park
- www.dachshundfriendshipclub.com
- Two gatherings, one in spring and one in fall; check website for schedule
- Transport: A, B, C, D, E, F and M trains/W 4 St; N and R trains/8 St – NYU

Wiener invasion

There is no animal on earth better than a dachshund. This is what dachshund owners believe, and if you come to one of their strange conclaves in Washington Square (the Dachshund Spring Fiesta in April or Dachtoberfest in October), you may actually start agreeing with them. "The dachshund is kind of a humorous dog for many people," says event founder Adrian Milton, slightly sad about that common defect. "But they're very dignified." His own dog Waldo perches in his arms with practiced nonchalance as it monitors the throng gathered between the arch and the fountain in Washington Square Park. "He's like a sphinx," says Milton.

One dachshund is cute; two is a little funny; two hundred in one place is surreal. The event has taken over the park, and whether the dogs themselves are aware of anything out of the ordinary is hard to gauge, although they do seem to enjoy the universal butt-snout parity as they greet each other. The breed has more variation within it than any other, so while the sausage profile is constant, you can get any color from blonde to caramel to black, or spots of all that, and coats that range from silky to wiry. It's bad form to laugh when you're told, as you soon will be, that dachshunds were bred for hunting. Particularly since it's true: the name means "badger hound" in German, and the standard of the breed is larger and more muscled than the glad-eyed lapdogs that waddle around your ankles. "Once you see the standard, you can begin to understand how they could take on a badger," says a guy wearing a tee-shirt bearing the slogan I KNOW A LITTLE GERMAN. "There's one right there! See? He's very powerfully built." Power is relative, of course; in the mix of dogs there's an incongruous beagle on a leash whipping its head around excitedly, stunned by this windfall of unfamiliar dominance.

Every owner is proud, but the ones here seem to have come less to reinforce what they already know—that dachshunds are simply superior—than for the benefit of the pets themselves. It's in keeping with how the whole event got off the ground. "We started twenty-one years ago," says Milton. "We rescued a dachshund who had a brother that was run over by a car, and every time he'd see another dachshund he'd start moaning. So we put a sign on a telephone pole, picked a date, and about fifty people showed up. Then it just grew and grew."

ANTHROPOMORPHIC MOUSE TAXIDERMY

Offered through the Observatory, Brooklyn
• See website for schedule and locations: www.observatoryroom.org
• Class fee: $100 (includes mouse)

> *Stuffed,*
> *with whimsy*

When you arrive at a class in anthropomorphic mouse taxidermy—which may be worth taking just to savor how those words hang together—you are confronted with a long table, and on it several dead mice to choose from. The animals have been … "saved" is not quite the term. They've been shifted, in destiny, from a snake food outfit in the Midwest. Those curious about taxidermy but squeamish about murder will be pleased to know: they arrive pre-dead. "I don't put in any request for color or size or anything," says class leader Divya Anantharaman. "It's a natural product, so you never know."

The concord with "natural" largely ends after you select a mouse and go to work on it. Anantharaman offers her classes through the Brooklyn Observatory, which has cornered an interest in stuffing animals (you might also get inside squirrel, guinea pig, or English sparrow), although the interest is actually a revival: the style of taxidermy offered can be traced back to a 19th-century craft sensation with the suspiciously cheery name "Victorian whimsy." A squirrel mounted on a branch studying an acorn is taxidermy. Give it a pipe, a tiny cup of tea, and a deck of cards, and you've got whimsical.

To arrive there, you have to go through a bit of yuck. You could do the whole operation at your own kitchen table: all you'd really need is dry preservative, a sharp knife, needle and thread, and a tendency not to throw up a lot. But you'll want Anantharaman around for the trickier moves like tongue and brain removal, or figuring out what to keep (skin, skull, paws and forelimbs, tail) and what to toss (everything else).

The class has a variety of props you can choose from, but the best results flow from personal visions. Aaron, who trekked all the way from Connecticut, has brought along a tiny bronze shield and sword, and a bristling crest. "It's deer fur," he says. "It just … seemed right." Not everyone puts in the thought necessary to skirt the clamoring indignity of dolling up a creature that might otherwise be scooting among the leaves of a chirping forest somewhere. "It's different every class," says Anantharaman. "Some people go for something really dynamic, some people are more subtle." A suggestion: go subtle.

BROOKLYN GRANGE

37–18 Northern Boulevard, Queens
• www.brooklyngrangefarm.com
• Farm open to visitors Saturdays 10 am – 3 pm (spring to fall)
• Transport: E and M trains/36 St

> ### *The good earth, overhead*

Brooklyn Grange is a farm on a roof. Most visitors access it through a café at street level which has its fruits and vegetables delivered, perhaps uniquely, from upstairs. When a waiter passes with a mixed salad, the owner says, "Yep," and points at the ceiling. "Everything on that plate came from up there."

The old six-story building, formerly a manufacturing plant, is square and sturdy, and has a footprint that is, as if an agricultural future were glimpsed in the architect's dream, almost exactly one acre. There are a few similar buildings on Northern Boulevard left over from a heyday in car building. Only this one has orderly rows of soil—over a million pounds of it—on top. There's also a chicken coop, beehives, wildflowers, and a small stand where you can buy the farm's produce: tomatoes, lettuce, kale, peppers, ground cherries, garlic. It's not a gimmick: the aerial field, created in 2010, is sustainable and even profitable. Rooftop farms work.

"We use this mixture called Rooflite," says Bradley, the farm manager, scooping up a handful of earth specked with flinty rock. "It's a good growing medium because it's got these porous stones." Not that weight is an issue: the industrial roof, which was specially prepared with layers of absorbent felt and runoff collecting measures, could withstand four times as much. The soil is enriched with compost; the farm creates its own with a solar-powered system. You can see how this works yourself on any Saturday during the growing season (spring to fall), and aside from the peculiar charm of taking an elevator to a tended field, you'll find it worth visiting for the view. The Manhattan skyline dominates the horizon; the city grid and the orderly rows of vegetables turn out to be a natural match.

The Grange has a companion project in the Brooklyn Navy Yard, and together they're the largest rooftop farms in the world. While you're stooped

over weeding or picking turnips, you might forget that you're 100 feet up. "It's funny, yeah," says Bradley. "Oftentimes I don't look at this all day"—motioning towards a glittering cityscape that includes the Citigroup Tower, the Empire State and Chrysler buildings. "Then, I love it when everybody goes home at the end of the day and I have time to myself with the plants and check out the view as the sun goes down."

HOLOGRAPHIC STUDIOS

240 East 26th Street
• www.holographer.com
• 212.686.9397
• Admission: free
• Open Monday to Friday 2 pm – 6 pm
• Transport: 6 train/23 St or 28 St

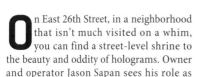

Light waves and lasers

On East 26th Street, in a neighborhood that isn't much visited on a whim, you can find a street-level shrine to the beauty and oddity of holograms. Owner and operator Jason Sapan sees his role as part artist, part educator, part secret wizard. "We've been here for forever," he says. "People just don't know about us." The best way to chance on the gallery might be after hours: in the display window there's a pool of electric light, and within it an exotic temple suddenly warps into being. Three feet tall, fully dimensional and brushed with shifting spectrums, as you walk by, the temple, or the mirage of it, tracks with your passing eye. "It's something I made for the Sultan of Brunei," Sapan says evenly, as though this were a fairly common thing.

For a fee Sapan will make a custom hologram for you, or reveal how you can design your own. During gallery opening hours, you can browse enough of these eerie 3D works to make you cross-eyed for a week. Holograms are illuminated starkly with crisp shadows, but there's a gloomy quality to the brightness, as though the objects were filmed by moonlight. It's never very hard to believe that they were created in Sapan's black basement, where, if you score a private tour, you'll see lasers and mirrors, and stands and contraptions bolted together, and a lot of electrical cable, and a skull, and a statue of an eagle, and developing bins, and four tons of other stuff. From this mess come neatly printed, strangely powerful illusions. A hologram's depth is so convincing, when you hold one in your hand it seems something has gone awry in your brain. It doesn't matter that the medium was invented decades ago: this is some of the witchiest tech going.

Sapan has made works of and for celebrities (on the wall a floating Andy Warhol watches you laconically as he leafs through a magazine), and tries to extend the art. He sees light as a medium of storage, likening holography to making a mold of a tire track in the mud, but instead of plaster you pour in light. "The thing with holography is—everything is there! It isn't just a trick medium. There's no bullshit. Everything is there, down to the size of a light wave." This truth is powerfully demonstrated in a series of holograms of microscopes; not only do the barrels of the eyepieces extend convincingly into space, when you look down them you can see the magnified objects at the other end of a lens that doesn't exist.

MUSEUM HACK

- www.museumhack.com
- 212.203.2729
- Check website for schedule
- Held at: Metropolitan Museum of Art
1000 Fifth Avenue
- Transport: 6 train/77 St; 4 and 5 trains/86 St/B and C trains/81 St (walk through Central Park)

Museum as fine dining experience

The Metropolitan Museum has six times as much art as the Louvre. It spans 5,000 years of creative history, covers 2 million square feet, and is visited by 137 quazillion people a year, most of whom seem to have shown up on the day you decide to go there yourself. "There's no way to see it in a few hours," says Mark Rosen, guide for Museum Hack. His solution: don't try. "You should treat a museum like you do a fine dining experience," he says to a group gathered in the museum's Great Hall. "What we want to do is show you our version of the tasting menu: the craziest, sexiest, coolest, weirdest things that you'd probably never think that this place has."

This, then, is "hacking": using the august grounds of the Met as a portal to more personal, and in some cases highly individual sights. If you do this already as a matter of habit, you might not need the reminder, but it's informative to see someone else's list of strange hits. Take the rococo interior in the European Decorative Arts wing; among the preserved furniture and paneled walls, there's a strange little structure in turquoise velvet and trimmed in gold. It's a dog kennel. What's more, it's the kennel of Marie Antoinette's toy spaniel Thisbe. What's even more, this was the same freaked-out Thisbe she was carrying on her glum march to the guillotine. "The dog survived," notes Rosen. Among the American portrait miniatures—tiny, sometimes incredibly detailed watercolor paintings on ivory—there is a pastoral scene fashioned entirely from human hair. Many Met lovers will be surprised to learn that there's a section called Visible Storage where objects not on official show are lined up on miles of shelves, like the world's most fascinating IKEA. Rosen navigates this warren to an "easy chair" made in Philadelphia around 1800. The tag notes the "mahogany and pine with original muslin-covered foundation," but skips the most arresting detail: a tin chamber pot connected under the seat. The chair is a plush, wing-backed toilet. Rosen: "A Met publication says that many if not most easy chairs at this time had chamber pots."

Then it's off to one of the less familiar corners to wonder at a walking stick that transforms into a flute, that then further transforms into an oboe, and is made from a pearly striated substance. It's one of only two intact narwhal-tusk musical instruments in the world. Think about that for a second. Then come back another day to see Van Gogh's cypresses or the temple of Dendur.

DEAD HORSE BAY

Southern side of the peninsula where Flatbush Avenue ends at the southeast corner of Brooklyn
• Transport: cyclists should take the bike trail that parallels Flatbush Avenue (east side), cross at Aviation Road and follow the trail into the bay

> *What is durable in life: seashells, shoe soles, and glass*

Dead Horse Bay is a curve of sand about a mile long at the southeastern tip of Brooklyn. Starting in the 1850s, the marshes here teemed with rendering plants: expired horses in steady supply were delivered from all over the city, chopped up, and boiled to make glue. Today you can walk the shore and still see hundred-year-old bones. But the better reason to make the trip to this weird bay is the vast collection of old garbage that litters it. When cars took over New York the rendering trade dwindled, and instead Dead Horse began a career as landfill. Picking your way over the tinkling beach, you soon learn what is durable in life: seashells, shoe soles—and glass.

You could call it a beach filled with bottles, but that doesn't quite cover the phenomenon. When the tide's out, there are stretches where you walk on a wet, crunching carpet of solid glass. Some of it is old and rare; as you crash around, you might wonder at every step if you've just destroyed the showpiece of some poor obsessive's collection. Now and then you can find small bottles in a hard-packed sediment of what must be mineralized trash; they crumble out like jewels from rock. Not all the glass is a bottle: the breakage makes objects mysterious. Bulbous forms, arcs, jug handles with no jug attached. Sometimes you'll spy what you think is the shoulder of an interesting find, only to discover that it's *only* the shoulder: kick it and it comes up, a shard hairy with algae, from the sucking muck.

With a little info, even the shards are interesting. A collector from Ontario holds a piece up to the sky and squints through it. "It's uranium glass," she says. "Shops used to give it out as promotions during the Depression." The shard still has the embossed ribbons and festoons meant to brighten the day of a vanished era. The color is pale chartreuse, and the glass really does contain uranium: held under a UV lamp, it will glow.

"What led us out here," says Caroline from Brooklyn, plodding over the beach in rain boots with her husband and two children, "was we heard that there's *so much* garbage left. But," wondering at a sea of glass, "I didn't expect the *mass* of it." If you've ever generated trash yourself—and of course you have—Dead Horse Bay can become a venue of reflection. "It's the fact that this is a place that was left," Caroline says. "We need to remember, on some level, that this is us. It's a cross section of us."

GARDEN SAGE
SALVIA OFFICINALIS MEDITERRANEAN REGION

FRAGRANCE GARDEN AT BROOKLYN BOTANIC ㉝

1000 Washington Avenue, Brooklyn
• www.bbg.org
• 718.623.7200
• Hours vary by season: see website

For best results, close your eyes

The Fragrance Garden in the Brooklyn Botanic was created for the nose, which generally doesn't get much special entertainment. It's an interesting question how many blind people take advantage of it, but without a doubt the provisions made for them—bronze identifying tags in Braille, and of course the choice and arrangement of plants—bring about in the rest of us a gentle mental shift. Here you can close your eyes and actually have a *more* intense experience.

The sense of smell has a noted power on the emotions, attributed to the proximity of the olfactory bulb to the brain's limbic system, where feelings and memories freely swirl. Many of the plants in the Fragrance Garden are compelling for suggesting smells that you already carry in your mind. Around the perimeter are large pots, each with several plants on a theme. One pot, tagged "Lemonade," has several citrusy species that evoke and are named after the lemon: lemon verbena, variegated lemon thyme, lemon bergamot. "Gently touch a leaf and smell the fragrance that rubs off onto your fingers," says the sign. "Does it smell good to you?" Yes. But when you sample one plant, lemon-scented geranium, your fingers smell not just like citrus, but—exactly, distinctly—lemonade. And not even natural lemonade: it's a dead ringer for the cheap, strong, artificial kind that comes in a foil packet and has a chemical aftertaste you could still detect from lunch while weed-whacking around the fence posts on a late summer afternoon when you were 13.

Where the garden might be content to keep pulling this evocative trick—you'll find plants that smell like root beer, pineapple, peppermint candy, almond, coconut, marshmallow—it goes further in explaining how the fragrances got there to begin with. When we toss rosemary in the sauce, the spice seems to have been created just for the certain zing it adds to our recipes. But when we exploit plants for special aromas and flavors, we're coming in at the end of a long, slow saga of secret chemical warfare. What teases our human brain might fry another. Even happy lemon is in on the game. "Some plant fragrances," says the sign, "act as self-defense. Lemon-scented plants have been known to keep away fleas, mosquitoes, ants and even cats." Knowing a thing like that makes the world a stranger place.

DUMPSTER DIVING WITH THE FREEGANS

• Check website calendar for meetings and trash tours:
www.freegan.info
• Once a month, the group prepares foraged food at a communal feast

> **It's a free market**

A freegan is someone who, wholly or in part, gets their food from the garbage. The first time you hear the term, the resonance with "vegan" is usually good for a titter, as though there's a natural continuum that starts with cutting out the red meat and ends glumly munching in an alley from a Hefty bag. But the difference between food and trash is the distance from a market's door to the sidewalk. If you want to learn the freegan arts, join any of the regular "dumpster dives" around the city.

"Try to postpone your gratification," jokes group organizer Janet on a recent circuit of Brooklyn Heights, "until you get home and you can see what you're eating." This is wise: the major drawback of dumpster diving, aside from filth, is how freakish any food looks under street lamps. But freegans aren't grazers, they're foragers: they find food that is perfectly acceptable, and prepare it, just like humans typically will, in a kitchen somewhere. "It's a hunt," says Jenny, a young lady who says she hasn't spent a penny on food for over a month.

You take whatever you can get, which means whatever the markets happen to be discarding that day. The mystery makes opening and rifling through trash bags strangely exciting. "I feel like a kid," says a first-timer, hauling out an armful of mustard greens. "Does anybody want a broccoli?" he says. "Apples?" Tim, a tall guy with a beard and a camping-style backpack that he may or may not be living out of, smiles quizzically at a plastic tub. "This is something I've never seen outside of the trash, actually," he says. "Pineapple cottage cheese? I didn't know they made that." The group, about two dozen strong, is friendly and high-spirited, which seems to puzzle some passersby. "What the *hell*," says a teen thudding by with a basketball. "It's garbage!" "Have you looked at the food that I got?" asks a freegan. "Yeah. From the garbage!"

"If he stayed around to listen," says tranquil Janet, "I'd tell him that half of our country's food is being thrown out. When you picture the big scale, it's sickening and what we're doing is a tiny drop in the bucket. But at least it's in the right direction. Here, this is for you," she says, pressing into your correspondent's hand an unbroken bar of imported chocolate, clean and on the right side of the expiration date. "Reassuring, isn't it?" she says. "It's the shittiest stuff you could eat, compared to the produce. But it feels safer."

THRILLS

POLAR BEAR PLUNGE

Coney Island Boardwalk
• Annually, January 1
• The Polar Bear Club swims throughout the winter; check website:
www.polarbearclub.org
• Transport: D, F, N and Q trains/Coney Island – Stillwell Av

Looking the coming year in the face

Jumping into the Atlantic Ocean in the middle of winter sounds like a bad idea. And it is. It's a supremely bad idea. This is why people come to take part in the Polar Bear Plunge, held at Coney Island every year. If it were especially smart or easy, there would be no point.

"It's like looking the coming year in the face and saying: I got you," says one of a group of shivering men from Maspeth, Queens, waiting on the boardwalk before the mad rush down the beach and into the freezing ocean. "It's mainly for the fun," says another. They are interrupted by what you may assume is their chief: a swaggering bear of a man who sports a terrycloth robe, a dozen Mardi Gras-style beaded necklaces, a stocking cap, and a bushy beard flecked with snot. "Look," he says with a beer-scented growl. "Look. If we don't have a heart attack, we get to live another year. If we drop dead, our problems are over. Happy New Year."

Togetherness is the theme of the event, and many attendees come in teams: groups united by costumes or neighborhood. The crowd is, it seems, entirely New York City; insane bravado is not on the tourist agenda. Many are repeat swimmers. "You do it the first year and you think: that was amazing," says Matthew from Brooklyn. "And every year on the train ride down you think: why am I doing this again? It's freezing. But confronting this with a bunch of people makes it better."

The event is sponsored, and it may be one undertaking where the level of control and organization goes totally unresented, although you're as likely to find anxiety as reassurance in the collection of ambulances that flank the boardwalk entrance, and the small Coast Guard fleet out on the dead grey ocean. And in fact, the experiences leading up to the heart-stopping plunge are the real torment: it's already so cold out in the air, as soon as you've dived in the water, your frail body seems beyond caring. Screaming seems to help (there's a lot of screaming).

"It's an exhilly, unh-ex*hi*larating experience!" says dripping John Esposito, a Coney Island native. "It's great going in, great feeling it. One of the top New York traditions. Par-puh-party of the *year*, that's it."

NEW FULTON FISH MARKET

800 Food Center Drive
- www.newfultonfishmarket.com
- 718.378.2356
- Open Monday to Friday 1 am – 7 am
- Transport: Bx6 bus/Food Center & National Food

> *The country's largest fish market*

The old Fulton Fish Market was on the shore of the East River just south of the Brooklyn Bridge, and for well over a century spiced downtown with the racket of mongers, the stink of the sea, and the Mafia. It was the last outdoor market of any significance in Manhattan, and visiting according to its graveyard schedule was a favorite activity among night owls with a yen for the hectic. The New Fulton Fish Market, built in 2005, is even larger, but you have to weigh your interest against the enormous pain in the ass of getting there. The industrial flats of South Bronx are tough during the day; at four in the morning they're downright ominous. But that's when New Fulton is hopping. New York's restaurants and retailers send out armies to buy meat and produce while the city sleeps.

The market is a single, vast hangar: the largest wholesale fish outfit in the nation. It might also qualify as the largest refrigerator. It's always cold here; the guys wear hip boots and wool caps and gloves, and shift cardboard boxes full of ice and pollock, or wrestle out chilled swordfish onto tables. There is a swagger to the workers—most have a wicked steel fishhook balanced on their shoulder—that seems out of place under the endless rows of fluorescent light, because it really belongs to the sea. The fish business remains wild: the supply chain, unlike one that leads from a ranch or a farm, is unknowable. "It's been windy up and down the coast," says seller Bobby Weiss, noting a meager catch this early Friday morning. "The wind is a lot more of a factor than the weather—it's all about the wind direction. Shark's one seventy-five," he says to a buyer (all Fulton conversations are friendly, and all eventually get cut off like this).

A walk down the vast length of the hangar is an obstacle course of crates, loading palettes, sodden cardboard, baskets, and small hills of crushed ice. At every moment, brightly colored forklifts veer and vroom, bearing boxes of seafood or heading off to the truck docks to load up. Tuna from Central America. Kingfish from the Gulf. Oysters from New Zealand. It's a machine with a million parts; the entire world leads to it. And it's a little more interesting for being so vast and at the same time so hidden from the rest of Metropolis.

CHRISTIE'S AUCTIONS

Christie's New York
20 Rockefeller Plaza
• www.christies.com/locations/salesrooms/new-york
• 212.636.2000
• Transport: B, D, F and M trains/47 – 50 Streets – Rockefeller Cntr

> *A sport of art and commerce*

Christie's auctions are open to the public, and there are more than a few reasons to go see one. Fine auction houses are like museums where everything is for sale, and if you need a brush-up on the cold truths of how art and commerce scratch each other's backs, an auction will set you straight immediately. The objects exhibited in the viewing rooms—a sort of artwork purgatory—display projected prices on the title card. The work might be a masterpiece, and here you're offered a glimpse as it passes, after an exchange of lucre, from one sitting room or safe to another. Check the calendar, choose an area that interests you—rare wines, Chinese ceramics, post-Impressionists—and enjoy the spectacle for what it is: part gallery, part boxing ring.

"Seventy-five thousand," says the auctioneer. "A rather incredible painting, to say the least! Seventy-five thousand," he repeats, "And now seventy-eight thousand—thank you sir! Eighty thousand?" The salesroom is plain: gray walls, rows of chairs with an aisle in the middle. Large monitors display on one side an image of the lot up for bid, and on the other the rising number in dollars, with the rest of the world's major currencies ticking up below. These numbers have a mesmerizing power: they're the province of human chaos, but gently intensified by the auctioneer, whose expert performance is an attraction of its own. He holds a pen in one hand and a small gavel in the other, and when the bids have stalled he leans out eagerly, peering over his glasses: it's at the same time chummy and authoritative. His hands come together in a formation that looks like prayer. "Are you sure?" he asks. "Sebastian?" he says to one of the telephone bidders standing along the walls. "Bidder online," he says, glancing into the ceiling where a camera has connected the salesroom to the entire globe, "are you sure? Fair warning!" Then the hands drop: the gavel raps down, and all the contingencies evaporate. The final number on the screen has become fate.

Later, asked what it's like to be up there, regular Christie's auctioneer James Hastie says, "It's very rewarding and enjoyable, actually. But never forget: they're throwing money at you! And if you like people and you get into the action, and you get a full crowd, it just makes for a very fun experience."

RACING CLUB NYC

- www.rcnyc.net
- Track located off Bronx Boulevard, on the left immediately after passing under East Gun Hill Road (heading south)
- Transport: 2 and 5 trains/Gun Hill Rd

A small-car culture

A t the Gun Hill Road elevated train station, you can look out west and not have a clue that a river runs through the Bronx. It's down under the trees: you can walk along it, and canoe it (see page 147), and, as in the case of Fort Knox Park, discover an entire culture on its banks. For over thirty years, both officially and not, lovers of radio-control have been raising dust here on a small shoulder of land. Come on practically any weekend from spring to fall, and you'll find cars no more than 2 feet long ripping around a well-tended course of jumps and switchbacks, Barbara, watching lazily from a bench, explains. "Most people don't know this is here. Most people don't venture outside of their *door*, actually." If that's you, you've just been reproached by a woman who sips her beer from a paper bag.

The cars have internal combustion engines powered by nitro. "The piston's like the size of a dime," says Dave Amaru, here from Long Island for a monthly club race. "But they make almost three horsepower." They also make the sort of noise that thrills a gearhead's ear: the howl of controlled explosions. It's the reason this track is the only one in the five boroughs. "New York don't like the noisy shit, you know?" says Amaru with an uncomprehending shrug. His own car lies in pieces on a folding table; he points out the miniature parts: fuel tank, engine, the servos that control throttle and steering. A chassis alone costs nearly a thousand dollars, which is why you don't see a lot of kids up on the stage where controllers, like looming gods, thumb their remote units as the cars skid around the sculpted hills below. "Yeah, it's always been an adult sport," says J. Armwood, president of the Radio Club of New York. "If you're a kid, it's difficult to get into if your dad doesn't do it, so it's more of a father–son thing." He pauses. "Or just a father thing."

Not to say that kids don't like it: they're entranced by small cars that work just like big ones. Some are recruited to dart out onto the course and set the machines back on their wheels when they've flipped over and suddenly become, despite a screaming engine, as feckless as turtles. Accidents? "You can get a flameout," says Amaru, referring to a torched motor. Generally the crashes have no effect: a group of cars can hardly make a lap without at least one launching from a jump at an angle and whipping pinwheels off the course and into the weeds. Once it's back on the track it takes off with a tail of dirt, buzzing and leaping again at 40 miles an hour.

MOUNTAIN BIKING AT CUNNINGHAM PARK

Bounded by 73rd Avenue, Francis Lewis Boulevard, and 210th Street
• www.nycgovparks.org/parks/cunninghampark
• 718.217.6452
• Transport: F train/179 St; park is approx. twenty minutes north by bike
Important: the biking trailhead at 210th Street and 67th Avenue is the only convenient entrance

Natural thrills

After mastering the lethal surprises of the street—potholes, wrong-way deliverymen, texting pedestrians—the New York cyclist may still hanker for more, and different, excitement. Try roots, poison ivy, and jutting rock. "I can't believe they fit all that in one place," says one mountain biker, panting at the trailhead of Cunningham Park after grinding out a few laps around the main course. It's only a couple of miles, but there seems to be a strange amount of wild in it. Lush brambles and bush line a narrow ribbon of packed dirt that dips and climbs, and ducks under canopies formed by fallen trees, and bumbles over boulders. And the principal course, rated for beginners (and ridable with a street bike), is just one of many: from and through it wind gnarlier, expert-level options. They have names: Iguana, Ringer, Viper. The more a track sounds like a piece of military hardware, the more you'll need the right kind of bike, and a helmet, and thrill issues.

Every crossing is marked by a signpost bearing difficulty ratings according to sport standards, from mellow green to demonic black diamonds ("Full face helmet and body armor required"). A rider might as easily want simply to fly through some stunning and unexpected nature. Cunningham Park is a marvel. That strip of dirt becomes mesmerizing as it wends through a rush of varied green: tall thin trees rocking in the breeze, wildflowers crowding either bank, humps of ivy concealing rotting logs, and sunbeams piercing the canopy, each one seemingly pre-scattered with its own dizzy gnats and butterflies.

A HISTORIC RIDE
The other reason to get your bike out to Cunningham Park is the stretch of Vanderbilt Motor Parkway that runs from the park's eastern edge to Winchester Boulevard. Built in 1908 by William K. Vanderbilt II, great grandson of Cornelius Vanderbilt and pioneering auto racer, the Parkway was the world's first long-distance road made exclusively for cars. The Grand Prix races held here attracted enthusiasts from all over the world. Today it's a mile of paved elevated road through trees with gentle hills: one of the best bike rides in the city.

BOULDERING IN MANHATTAN

- Gareth Leah's website: www.nycbouldering.com
- His book: *NYC Bouldering* (Sharp End Books, 2013)

> *A sport with a bit of kick*

Metropolis might at first seem to be short on rugged ingredients—rock faces, cliffs, massive boulders—but in fact it has all that. Not as dramatically as say, Utah, but certainly enough to make climbing your sport without ever leaving the island. Bouldering, or scaling rock without a belay rope, has decades of tradition in New York. Writer and adventurer Gareth Leah recently compiled over 300 routes in *NYC Bouldering*, a book that aims to be the encyclopedia of Manhattan's natural crags, cracks, and ledges.

Leah recently took a morning to show one of his favorite spots, a little-known face at the northern edge of High Bridge Park dubbed Waldo Rocks. "It's because everyone always asks where it is," he says, unfolding a crash pad on the ground and slipping into a pair of dirty climbing shoes. "It's so pathetic, but it's funny." Leah is from Chester in the U.K.; he's young, scruffy, and radiates a wholesome self-sufficiency. His bona fides are visible: he has the trim build and ropey forearms, but also an interesting scar on his cheek owed to a climbing accident in the Middle East ("A rock fell on me, and my jaw," pointing up at his ear, "came through my face"). He rubs chalk on his hands and explains the sport's appeal. "It's kind of like cycling or running," he says. "You enjoy moving and the adrenaline that goes with it, but rather than going in a straight line, you're going up. I guess there's also the thrill factor of the fall and the danger involved—it's just a sport with a bit of kick." He points out a good route, a crack offering a few "jugs," or deep, easy holds, and then wrestles his way up in a series of controlled moves. You'll find when you take a firm hold that schist has a sharp tooth and glitters with crystal. Pulling yourself up a vertical rock face in the green light of a forest morning, even with the traffic of Dyckman Boulevard only a few yards away, will make you feel close to Manhattan in a peculiarly vivid way.

Clambering on city structures is a recognized sport, too: it's called "buildering." But New York is no place to do it. "Everyone's afraid to get sued," says Leah. Not that permission is exactly required. He has ascended, for example, the stanchions of the Williamsburg Bridge. "Easy. It's jugs all the way up."

GARETH LEAH'S LIST OF TOP FIVE MANHATTAN BOULDERING SPOTS

Rat Rock, Central Park
Worthless Boulder, Central Park
St. Nich's Wall, St. Nicholas Park
Flying Squirrel Rock (Waldo), High Bridge Park
Sherman Boulders, Fort Tryon Park

NORTH BROOKLYN BOAT CLUB ❹①

Entrance: 49 Ash Street at McGuinness Boulevard, Brooklyn
• www.northbrooklynboatclub.org
• Membership dues: $40/year
• Regular free paddles in kayaks and canoes as well as other events; check website for schedule
• Transport: 7 train/Vernon Blvd – Jackson Av; G train/Greenpoint Av

Inviting and gritty

For a general sense of what it's about, the best way to approach the North Brooklyn Boat Club is walking over the Pulaski Bridge from Queens. The feeling is: this is a landscape where urbanity won. Rail yards, tollbooths, tunnels, every kind of concrete, steel stanchions and trusses, fences topped with barbed wire. Then, down below on the Greenpoint side of Newtown Creek, you see a well-tended strip of alley that leads to a floating platform and, scattered in the dark water around it, brightly colored kayaks.

The club, which has nearly 200 paying members, keeps its boats in corrugated shipping containers, that emblem of reclaimed design, and you get to it through an entrance cloaked in morning glories and banked by a neat garden bed full of butternut squash. It didn't get this way by itself. "This was covered in weeds, and just junk, and old trucks," says Scott Behr, a club member whose metal shop is down the street. "I kept seeing it get cleaned up, so I just came down here one day and was like: What are you guys *doing*? And they said: It's a boat club!"

In the city you can take a canoe down an idyllic river (see page 147), or among islets in a bay (see page 107): here you row to discover the dirty, enveloping, magnificent city. Inland is New York's main water treatment facility and the still waters of Newtown Creek, which is more off-putting either for the millions of gallons of oil spilled there over the years, or for the raw muck that flows into it from the city's sewers—hard to say. West lies the fast and wild tidal estuary of the East River and the iconic skyline. Figuring out your place among these forces is part of getting out in this water. Members take off alone; visitors paddle in groups. Watching Manhattan grow slowly larger as massive barges slide past the unpretty face of the industrial shorefront, and hard-ass tugboat workers grin and raise their gloved thumb at you, you'll feel connected to the city's very guts.

In the afternoon, founding member Fung Lim starts a fire in the club's brick pit and makes popcorn in a stock pot. Lanky and smiling, with a black ponytail and the hands of somebody who knows his way around a toolbox, Lim has helped form the club's unique vibe: inviting and gritty. "It's not a Sunday picnic paddle on a nice calm lake," he says. "But people have to use something and appreciate it and have fun on it before they can say: this is mine. That's where we come in."

HIGH FALLS CLASS AT HOLLYWOOD STUNTS 42

73 West Street, Brooklyn
- www.hollywoodstunts.com
- 917.548.5461
- Classes offered on Saturdays; see website for schedule
- Transport: G train/Greenpoint Av

You're not supposed to feel comfortable

On the Greenpoint waterfront stand long, tall warehouses of weathered brick and corrugated tin; in one of them you can learn how to take a karate kick in the gut, or run around covered in flames, or crash through a shopwindow. This is Hollywood Stunts NYC, and founder Bobby Cotter (safe bet that the Porsche out front with license plate "STUNTBOB" is his) says that, as far as this kind of instruction goes, "We're the only ones in the city." Cotter has a lined face, a smoker's baritone, and the slow and steady manner of a guy who hasn't had to take any shit from anyone in a real long time. A working stuntman, when asked what his specialty is he growls, with no elaboration: "Fire."

The facility offers a full package of training, covering most of the mayhem required by the film industry. To give normal folks a taste of the life, the shop offers a High Falls class, which also advertises itself (optimistically) as roughshod therapy for people with a crippling fear of heights. There's a variety of falls; in class you'll be doing the misnamed "suicide," which involves not slumping into the void with a bottle of bourbon, but springing upward to gain height, tucking into a cannonball at the top of the arc, finding a visual mark on the ceiling, and then planking as flat as possible before you land, back-first.

"You're not supposed to feel comfortable with jumping and landing on your back," says instructor Zack. "So the first time's not going to be great." You practice first on a foam mat from a platform. One of the tips is to yell before you hit, expelling the air from your lungs and helping the body to relax. "You should just smack flat," says Kelvin, another instructor. "It should make one sound: _WHAP_." When everyone in the class has more or less got the whap, the guys unfold and inflate an enormous air bag.

You scale a narrow ladder, like a high diver, to an aluminum platform 30 feet up. Fed with constantly running fans, the puffy bag has a white square in the center; you might wonder what that square must look like to a professional standing on the edge of a building four times as high, in a heavy wind. "Bag's up!" yells Zack from below. "Clear to fall," says Kelvin at your side. The phrases are a safety ritual, and the next one is yours. "Falling," you say—and leap. The class lasts a couple of hours; after, when you gather your things to return to the normal world, there's a flutter in your chest as though you've just run a mile.

RAIL MEAT AT THE RARITAN YACHT CLUB

160 Water Street, Perth Amboy, New Jersey
- www.ryc.org
- 732.826.2277
- Racing season: May to October
- Transport: New Jersey Transit from Penn Station to Perth Amboy; the club is a ten-minute walk from the station, or call for a taxi: 732.826.7447

> **No experience necessary**

The Raritan Yacht Club, which is located in New Jersey but races in the waters of New York City's Lower Bay, has a friendly but fierce competitive season from May to October. On Wednesdays, dedicated yachters zigzag a miles-long course around the bay's markers and buoys. The ideally eight-man crews are nearly always short at least one person: for them a problem, for you an opportunity. On race days if you loiter at the club, in an uncreepy way, you'll be snapped up as "rail meat" or human ballast. The beauty: no experience necessary.

"It's like this," says Steve Scanlon, a man who is somehow sly, jolly and commanding at the same time, and one you'll be lucky to call skipper onboard his 29-footer, the *Mad Cow*. "This is the keel, and this is the rudder," lining his hands up like fins. "Too much angle, and instead of cutting, you drift. You gotta level her out. That's where rail meat comes in." The term, you'll gather, carries a whiff of derision. "It's lovingly derogatory," smiles Ruthie, Scanlon's better half. Another part of a first-time rail meat's job is absorbing a certain amount of terror; after hopping a launch out to the yacht ("Cows on, let's go!" cries Scanlon), the different parts of the boat that might kill you are helpfully pointed out. "When I yell 'Prepare to jibe,'" says the skipper, patting the boom or the horizontal bar of the mainsail, "pay attention or this thing's gonna take your head off." The jib sheet, the line connected to the front sail, "can knock you right over—or cut you in half."

The focusing power of these warnings is remarkable. And a good thing, because although rail meat's job is to sit on the high side, when the boat tacks the side switches, which means you have to be quick to crawl over the cabin top while the boom swings for your brains, and climb the suddenly heaving deck—all while the scenery of vying yachts and lighthouses abruptly spins to one side or the other. "The first time is going to feel crazy," says the mainsail trimmer.

It does. Scanlon shouts from the helm: "Ready about! Tacking in five, four, three, two … one!"—and everything on the boat goes wild: the sheets jump and writhe, the boom lunges, the jib sail roars. Then you're sitting safely on the opposite rail, buzzing with thrill as your feet hang above the rushing water, one member of a team whose pleasure is to harness the wind.

KAYAK IN JAMAICA BAY

Parks Department offers free instruction and kayaks
• For more freedom, Wheel Fun Rentals keeps kayaks at Riis Landing and Canarsie; rates: $15/hour, $30/half day;
www.wheelfunrentals.com/Locations/New-York-2

> **Out among forbidden isles**

The islands of Jamaica Bay are mysterious clumps of emerald marshland lying low out on the water. One of them, Broad Channel, harbors the Jamaica Bay Wildlife Refuge, which is the country's largest such refuge fully within city limits: 330 species of birds have been spotted there, or about half of all the species in the Northeast. The other islands are strictly forbidden. In 2007, *New York* magazine floated a reporter on a Crusoe-style survival mission to the largest of them: he sent out an SOS by text after one day. If you think you might do better, and know how to leave birds alone, enjoy. The way to get out is by kayak.

Voyaging under your own power, especially in a stealthy craft that connotes the Noble Savage, is good for a pretty visceral thrill of independence. Jamaica Bay is in the lee of the Rockaway peninsula of Queens so the water, except when combed out in the wakes of passing boats, is calm. There are dozens of islands, and while you're not supposed to set foot on them, many are squiggled with channels that you can explore. The shores of the larger ones are dotted with the wrecks of boats, as though a modest apocalypse has just occurred, but the low grassy islets are wonderfully wild, untouched, rimmed in mussels and thriving with birds. "You'll see the whole array," says Parks ranger John Daskalakis. "Gulls, geese, sandpipers, plovers. They give you this look like: *What are you doing in my place?*"

The most curious part about being out among the lonely marsh grass, listening to the cackle of seabirds, is looking beyond at a distant skyline that is as urban as it gets. Your phone still works. You can set the oar athwart the kayak, call your sister and describe the scene, then take a pic and send it to her, then check the map for the little blue dot of your present location: afloat in a channel twisting through a desert isle. Then slip overboard for a swim before paddling back.

NYPD RIDE ALONG

• Precincts are assigned by neighborhood; download the application at:
www.nyc.gov/html/nypd/downloads/pdf/community_affairs/
ridealong2013.pdf

The other side of the blue line

For the Ride Along program, where you accompany a pair of NYPD officers on their daily rounds, you arrive early in the morning and, first thing, get velcroed snugly into a bulletproof vest. While this happens, you might be aware of having crossed a line. For the next couple of hours, you'll be among the city's protectors. The world will look different.

The mobile patrol unit of today's Ride Along is manned by Officer Sanchez, a sharp Dominican lady with a quick smile and a manifest intolerance for nonsense, and her partner Officer Tomacruz, a trim Filipino with a controlled edge acquired during his years as a Marine. They're both smart and young, and seem a little apologetic that, in a city that averages over a murder a day, the likelihood of dramatic felonies today is very low. Their precinct is the peaceable 20th ("The Two-Oh") on the Upper West Side, and the first hour of prowling involves zooming through traffic with the siren's brief yelps and wails (as they're marked on the console), stopping drivers for minor infractions. If you get pulled over, Sanchez has these tips for you. "Don't call me sweetie, don't call me *mami*," she says. "And don't lie. I saw you talking on your cell phone behind the wheel. You say you didn't? Now you're testing my intelligence."

The radio chirps and the dispatcher crackles a report of "an EDP on Columbus and West Seven-One." An EDP is an emotionally disturbed person, a.k.a. crazy, and after this one turns out to be unproblematic ("Sometimes when a guy's yelling," says wise Officer Tomacruz, "it's just a guy yelling") there's a call for a "domestic" or couple's argument a dozen blocks uptown. It's the type of call that can get very ugly. "In an apartment," says Tomacruz, "you don't know *what's* in there. And tempers are already high." When the patrol car pulls up to a five-story on West 84th, it unfolds that Ride Along means following the officers up the stoop while the neighbors gawk, and trooping on into the stairwell where each floor's closed doors begin to look just a shade ominous. It turns out to be a tiff between new roommates, and after hearing the more unhinged of the two for a minute, Sanchez tells them to figure things out. Back on the street the call is demoted from a "domestic" to a "dispute" over the radio, and with a yelp the patrol car crosses the avenue and heads back to precinct. "You see people as they really are," says Sanchez. But it's hard to tell from her shrug how she feels about it.

TREE CLIMBING FOR ADULTS

New York Botanical Garden
• www.nybg.org/adulted
• Class fee: $135
• Transport: Metro – North Harlem local train/Botanical Garden Station;
B, D and 4 trains/Bedford Park Blvd

> *You've entered another realm*

"**T**rees move," says David Fedczuk, instructor at the New York Botanical Garden. "At the beginning it can be a little … unsettling." While he speaks, he leans back in a saddle harness to take up the flex in a rope tethering him to the top of an 80-foot oak. The branch shivers. Fedczuk wears a white tee-shirt, baseball cap and heavy hiking boots; if the straight-shooting attitude and scars on his forearms haven't convinced you yet, the fluid way he cinches himself up the rope to the tree's branching crown will make it clear: if you want to learn to climb a living tower, this is the guy. After zipping down again he unhooks from the line and looks around. "Who's next?"

The introductory class lasts all day, and it's assumed, very attractively, that this is your new thing. You'll get an overview of the gear—harness, helmet, ropes—and learn that tree climbing is entirely legal in national forests, and in a murky status everywhere else. Ideally, you should have permission. "But if you start going around and asking," says Fedczuk, "you're going to get a no. If you just go out and do it, nine times out of ten nobody's going to notice." If the prospect of using advanced methods to ascend into the cool green canopy is enticing, the thought of doing so furtively is doubly so. On the ground, though, it's a mostly technical exercise. Fedczuk explains the ingenious art of securing a throw-line to a high branch, an operation that might require launching the weight with an 8-foot slingshot (a "Big Shot"). The line is used to haul a cambium saver, a loop of webbing with metal rings on either side for the main rope to pass through so the bark remains unharmed. This is a detail, like a tree's movement, that brings home how curious it is to use a rock climber's gear to get up into a living thing.

Gripping the metal ascenders, and kicking from the massive trunk to keep steady, you haul yourself into a slowly opening view of one of New York's most beautiful places. On a clear autumn day the red oak blazes, and falling acorns snap through the branches, and although you can still hear the life of the ground, even 10 feet above it you'll feel you've entered another realm. Far below a Garden tram cruises smoothly by, and the passengers crane their necks to get a look, as though you're a charismatic animal in a safari. "You mean you can climb the trees?" gapes a woman strolling by with her son. "They teach people this?"

Yes.

ARTS / PERFORMANCE

BACH VESPERS AT TRINITY CHURCH

Holy Trinity Lutheran Church
65th Street and Central Park West
• www.bachvespersnyc.org
• 212.877.6815
• Admission: free
• Every Sunday; check website for program
• Transport: 1 train/66 St – Lincoln Center; A, B, C and D trains/59 St –
Columbus Circle

> *Come
> for the Bach ...
> stay
> for the Bach*

From 1723 until he died in 1750, Johann Sebastian Bach was the cantor of the principal churches of Leipzig, Germany. His cantatas were written to be heard in a devotional setting: once at morning worship and again in the evening. Today you'll be happy to listen to Bach anytime through headphones, compliments of modernity, but there is something to be said for context. The Holy Trinity Lutheran has it. For forty-five years this church has been transporting listeners to 18th-century Germany, offering Bach's music in regular Sunday performances as the genius himself would have known it.

"The unique thing that we're in a position to do is actually present the cantatas in their liturgical order," says Rick Erickson, Trinity's own cantor. "But people come for any number of reasons. Some for the music, some for the motet literature, some just like the candles and incense and chant." Erickson is an organist of celestial talent, and if there's anything in the world that will justify live liturgical music, it's this instrument that can make the floorboards tremble. "Every organist is a fanatical child of Bach," the cantor says, smiling at the leviathan toy he has to play with. Whether music is gospel is for you to judge. It sounds, as all Bach does, like the voice of vast and busy forces, deep in thought. The organ itself is not just one instrument but a potential infinity. By adjusting the stops, the player accesses different registers: fluting, humming, piping. More subdued pieces seem to travel via a submarine chortle, some sigh with breeze, others cut and blast like horns. There are moments when the reverberating notes hang in a sour tension that then resolves in a holy roar of perfection. This is singing architecture.

Before the cantata, the choir forms a procession and follows the swinging censer into the apse, arranging themselves around a small Baroque ensemble. Bach never played a piano, and you won't find one here. Harpsichord, recorder, viola da gamba: the instruments are from the period, an effect that is practical as well as historical. "Period instruments are lower," says the soprano soloist. "They're more mellow." Not that she needs much help: the internationally celebrated choir has mastered the angelic nuances, but can belt out a roar of its own.

IMPROV JAM AT THE UPRIGHT CITIZENS BRIGADE

48

UCB Chelsea: 307 West 26th Street
UCB East Village: 153 East 3rd Street
• www.newyork.ucbtheatre.com
• 212.366.9176
• Check website for schedule
• Admission: $5
• Transport: Chelsea: C and E trains/23 St; 1 train/23 or 28 St

*Students
of chaos*

L ive improv comedy is the adrenaline sport of theater: there's a hectic thrill that scripted arts don't deliver. The Upright Citizens Brigade hosts performances every evening; there's also a weekly free-for-all, the improv jam, where you, person who has no idea what this is all about, might end up on stage getting laughed at. Probably in a good way.

The people who thrive in this scene aren't the shameless extroverts you'd imagine—in fact the opposite. "It really tends to be people who are shyer," says Andy Bustillos, who works the desk. "There's a framework, and someone can guide you into it without you even knowing it." This guiding effect has a power that is sometimes perfectly mysterious, and one of the most interesting aspects of improv is how performers navigate the moving parts of a team of frantically spinning brains. They are less comedians than students of chaos.

The jam starts with hopefuls throwing their names into a bucket. If you get picked, you join a team that's made up of half experienced performers, and half bucket draws. With each wave of teams, a theme is called out at random from the audience—"birthday," "marmalade," "syphilis"—and the players set about wrangling it into scene. Gradually a comic alchemy takes effect: just a few minutes ago, a group of people were standing uncertainly on stage; now we've reached a place where a drug addict is trying to enjoy the Anne Frank museum, or a man is asking his wife: "Honey, why is there lipstick on the Rumba?"

"The basis of improv is that there are no bad ideas," says Keilana Decker, a UCB student. "Whatever anybody says, you have to be able to accept it and support it." This theme of support is the art's backbone. Given the format, the scenes that don't quite come off—the ones that drag in the bedlam, never resolving into comic focus—can be as instructive as the ones that shine. The golden ingredient isn't charisma. In fact, the performers who try to steal the show tend to wreck it. "The experienced improvisers," says Decker, "they've all cultivated that ability: they understand how to catch those moments between people." With some training, and some guts, you might find this worth figuring out yourself.

753

SINGLE FARE

- Location varies; check website: www.single-fare.com
- Exhibition held in mid-February

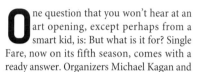

MetroCard art

One question that you won't hear at an art opening, except perhaps from a smart kid, is: But what is it for? Single Fare, now on its fifth season, comes with a ready answer. Organizers Michael Kagan and Jean-Pierre Roy state that they want to provide a setting "where art and artists can come together to form a monumental event." They can allow themselves to make grand claims like this. For one, they're probably right. For two, all of the artwork at Single Fare is 2 by 3 inches. That's the size of a standard MTA MetroCard subway pass which, according to exhibition rules, is the canvas the entries must be created on.

Each year the exhibition is held at a different venue; in 2013, RH Gallery on Duane Street was the place. On opening night there's a mob. The crowd spills off the stoop and into the street; people creep along the gallery walls to see the hundreds of tiny artworks. In the middle there's a general roil: artists, friends of artists, would-be collectors. Jean-Pierre Roy stands tall in the very center, visibly energized by the success. "You know, I think artists like it because it's very egalitarian," he says. "And every single piece is a hundred bucks. It's one of the few times actually that artists get to collect the work of their peers."

It's also one of the few times that artists all operate under the same constraint: each has had to reconcile the minuscule format with their technique. This makes for an atmosphere of good-natured competitiveness, and as they circle around, viewers hum with appreciation and pick favorites: the slashes and blots of abstracts, painterly portraits, film stills, mosaics made from chips of cards, even a spinning zoetrope. Certain artists achieve a lush, Ingres-like effect in miniature; in some works the ultrafine strokes have been applied with a single hair.

The uniformity of format can feed creativity. Artist Jane Lafarge Hamill, who ordinarily does large, physical paintings, had to buy new brushes and rethink her style. "It's an existential issue," she says. "If you have absolutely anything to pick from, what do you do? So, having a constraint can be really good for an artist. And seeing how everyone takes that in a different direction is inspiring."

FRIGID FESTIVAL

94 St. Marks Place and 85 East 4th Street
- www.frigidnewyork.info
- 212.777.6088
- Admission: $18
- Festival takes place in February

The city's only uncensored theater festival

New York City emits a searing amount of limelight, which grows gradually dimmer, and generally stranger, and potentially more intriguing the further it falls from Broadway. Nowhere is the glow more intimate than at the Frigid Festival, which takes place every winter in the East Village. Produced by the Horse Trade Theater Group and performed under St. Marks Church and in the creaky and enticingly dark theaters on East 4th Street, the festival offers thirty different hour-long performances from independent companies over the course of two weeks. What you can expect is: anything.

"There's no jury," says Lauren Arneson, a venue tech. "It's the only uncensored theater festival I've ever heard of in New York City." This wild card element is the core of Frigid's appeal, and the whole endeavor seems poised on the moment, say, when the kids notice that the school bus driver has just passed out. "If you give a structure," says Arneson, "but leave it open, it could be really amazing." She pauses. "It could also be a wreck. But then it will only be a sixty-minute wreck."

The performers are chosen by lottery, and aside from a stroke of luck, there's not much required. You get monologues, prop acts, physical comedy, general airings of sexuality and religion. In the 2013 program, John Grady's *Little Pussy* is a prodding of old wounds, asking with hilarious acuity what it means to behave like a man in a world bent on emotional destruction. The piece harnesses the power of a small stage: with only the slightest effects of lighting and sound, Grady's episodic shame shifts from a steamy high-school locker room to a blue-cold Toronto alley, to a patch of sidewalk under a New York streetlight. "When you get the chance to premiere a personal narrative like this," he says, "too often things get workshopped to death. But here you're not held back."

If you like this kind of thing, you'll like it more knowing that Frigid is also the only New York theater festival that gives the entire box office over to the performers. "Frigid wants to support artists," says Arneson. "If you give somebody a chance, they can create something great."

STRAD FOR LUNCH

W.M.P Concert Hall
31 East 28th Street
• www.wmpconcerthall.com
• www.gradouxmattrareviolins.com
• 212.582.7536
• Suggested admission: $10
• Concerts most Wednesdays at 12:30 pm; check online schedule
• Transport: 6 train/28 St; N and R trains/23 or 28 St

A luthier's private concert hall

As illustration of New York's inexhaustible capacity to surprise, take the twelve-story brick-and-stone building at 31 East 28th Street. Just around the corner from the roughest patch of midtown Broadway, and bookended by bars and bodegas, the address houses one of the world's great violin makers and repairmen. Emmanuel Gradoux-Matt, raised in Switzerland but based in the city for the last twenty-five years, is the person you see when your Stradivarius has a problem, or you're in the market for one, or you want to buy a new instrument made to the exacting sorcery of the old style. His shop is the kind of place that keeps its products in a walk-in safe in the basement.

Better than anyone, luthiers know that string instruments, for all their aura of transcendence, are just boxes made of wood and glue. They have to be played to come alive, and they have to be played regularly to stay brilliant. So Gradoux-Matt built himself a concert hall. "This used to be a furniture store," he says, indicating a small stage and room for an audience of about sixty-five. "Most of the chamber music played here—Beethoven, Brahms, Haydn, Mozart—was composed for small spaces like this one. Carnegie Hall is great, but it's not at all the musical experience that was intended." There's a genius to this: Gradoux-Matt has killed several birds with one stone. The rare violins get their exercise, the public gets the opportunity to experience the world's best instruments at just a few paces, the music is presented in its native setting, while the violin maker himself—arms folded, staring, critical—listens carefully.

"It is a tool," he says, "in the best way a tool can help craft something. One of the things that this allowed was to find great artists who never had the chance to do exactly what they want in a small concert hall. Some people come up with amazing stuff." You can listen for yourself on Wednesdays at 12:30. An instrument is pulled from the safe—it's almost always a Stradivarius—and played by a violinist of world caliber. It's the perfect experience for a music lover of an obsessive and fastidious bent because it was designed by one. As for the acoustics, Gradoux-Matt went with what he knew: the wood shell backdrop uses principles common in stringed instruments, creating a space that is a giant instrument in its own right.

PUNDERDOME 3000

- www.getyourcoatwereleaving.tumblr.com
- Check website for event schedule and location
- Admission: $7

> **New York's arena of wordplay**

Puns, as a form of humor, are cringing and oily: even the best ones carry a whiff of failure. When they're funny, the laughs are laced with groans. "A lot of people call it dad humor," says Joe Salgado, "and we definitely have it." He's one half, with his cousin Richy, of the Punder Twins, about to get on stage to do battle with rivals who have the same talent (or curse) at Punderdome 3000, New York City's unlikely arena of wordplay. In line are hundreds of enthusiasts who will cheer them on, or revel in their terribleness; many express a reluctant affection for the form. "I think it does speak to certain mental faculties," says Kate, a Punderdome regular. "It's really difficult to be on that stage." Asked if there's an identifiable punster type, she says, "You can't tell by looking at them. But within the first couple of seconds of the performance, you know."

This sudden knowing is part of the fun. Competitors are given a random theme; in ninety seconds they have to invent a set that will contain as much punning as possible. If this is a little goofy, it's also smart. And rooted: Shakespeare was a punster. James Joyce, too. In the first round the theme is "bakery," and after the unassuming Salgados rip off an opener full of stingers, Joe pauses for the shouts and laughter to tail off before adding: "We're already on a *roll*." If it's an art, here's an artist.

Punderdome is emceed by its creators, comedienne Jo Firestone and her father Fred. The concept was hers, the trappings his. Fred is a motivational speaker by profession. "I have a full game show set in my garage," he says, and this is enough to get a pretty good idea of him. Each event starts with Fred warming up the audience with a test of classic puns; then Jo explains the rules ("People who are funny get higher scores. That's a hint.") and the workings of the Applause-O-Meter, a blindfolded volunteer who tips the needle of a cartoonish headdress from 1 to 10 depending on the volume of hooting and clapping—which can get downright thunderous.

The best competitors manage somehow to address the theme and their own frailty before a crowd that freely blurs jeers and cheers. Punky Brewster (Do Pun to Others, Punder Express—they've all got names like this), a smallish young lady with a whipcrack brain, delivers some OK material on the theme of "poison," then, as if by apology, shrugs: "I'm doing *asbestos* I can." The crowd goes berserk, and Punky (who later sweeps the whole show) glows as she soaks up this rare dose of power and respect. For a punster, it's a home won.

OPEN STUDIO AT MAD

Museum of Arts and Design
2 Columbus Circle
• www.madmuseum.org/programs/open-studios
• 212.299.????
• Admission: free with museum ticket ($16, seniors $14, students $12)
• Open museum hours: Tuesday to Sunday 10 am – 1:30 pm
and 2:30 – 5 pm, Thursday and Friday 6 – 8:30 pm
• Transport: 1, A, C, B and D trains/59 St – Columbus Circle

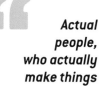

Actual people, who actually make things

The Museum of Arts and Design, NYC's center of all things applied arts, goes far in public outreach by making actual people, who actually make things, available to you. Stroll through the recent exhibit on woodworking—then hit the elevator to the glass cubicle on the sixth floor and watch chips fly as an artist in residence spins a block on a lathe. The artists cycle through the week, so the jewelry maker you see on Monday will be replaced by a knitter on Tuesday, and by a ceramicist on Wednesday, etc.

The glass cubicle is more than a little like an aquarium, and if the purpose weren't to foster contact between creators and the public, it would almost be inhumane. "It's more of a show and tell than just churning out work," says Ben Light, the woodworker. "You get used to it." Light rests one hand on a cylinder of poplar that is just beginning to show the basic curves of a lamp. His material is reclaimed wood, some of it turned whole on a lathe, some of it cut into precise combs that nest together in eye-catching masses. "I *think* I've invented this," he says. "It's taking a laser cutter, which is a relatively new technique, and turning, which is just about the oldest technology. It's sort of a 3D plywood." Light's woods have stories, and they're worth hearing in person: a polished lamp made from a stump that was submerged under a manmade lake for 150 years, and another cut from a plank of oak that was once part of a fermentation vat at a bourbon distillery (when you turn the lamp on, it smells like whiskey).

A few minutes before closing, a museum guide leads in a troupe of visitors. "The purpose of coming in here," she says, with a deferential smile for the rare animal inside, a Creator, "is so that your eye will begin to be attuned to techniques, and why artists spend their lives making art. When you go back down to the floor, you will understand: each piece represents a life." Two tots wearing oversized goggles stand at polite attention as the designer works a sharp file over the blur of spinning wood, his hands slowly buried in shavings. "What is wood made of?" asks Dad. "Cellulose," says the little girl. Light raises his eyebrows. "What's cellulose made of?" proud Dad persists, but the chemistry lesson devolves into a sawdust fight.

ST. THOMAS CHURCH CHOIR

1 West 53rd Street
• www.saintthomaschurch.org
• 212.757.7013
• Choir sings regularly during the school year for choral liturgies (Sundays 11:30 am) and choral evensong (Sundays 5:30 pm) as well as weekday evenings; check website for schedule. Free guided tours of the church building are offered after Sunday morning service
• Transport: E and M trains/53 St

> **The only residential boys' choir school in the country**

You can't exactly call the regular choral services of the St. Thomas Church choir "performances;" the talent is world-class, but the singing you get naturally from the fact that the church operates a school centered on the choral arts. During the academic year, you can attend on nearly any Sunday and hear the boys sing as adornment to the service.

"The feeling I have each September," hums the rector from the elevated pulpit on the first Sunday of the school season, "might be likened to the full throttle of a jet plane taking off. It's the sudden presence of a schoolful of third- to eighth-graders among us—learning, practicing, rehearsing, and performing—and over at the choir school it includes living, eating and sleeping, classes of all sorts, and innumerable school activities from playing an instrument to kicking a soccer ball." It sounds like a mix of Harry Potter and *The Name of the Rose,* and it's unique: St. Thomas is the only residential choir school left in the United States, and one of very few in the world. To sit in on the service is to witness a centuries-old tradition. "The miracle of music," the rector continues, "part of the the human person, is actually part of human transcendence."

What counts as transcendent varies; you'll have to suspend comment until you've heard what these kids can do. Backed up by professional adult singers—grayer, taller, and more near-sighted former boys—they add a note of cosmic beauty to the welling song, like the shimmer of strings. The boys take communion first, in order to be able to resume providing a glorious soundtrack for the rest of the faithful filing forward. It must be a powerful thrill to enter that gauntlet of astral sound and connect it, with a brimming heart, to the eternal. For the rest of us the astral sound is enough.

After service, the choir director and organist John Scott tears the place down with a raging, contemporary Duruflé toccata, and half the congregation heads back into the social room for coffee. The rector says that what he feels most from his association with the residential choir is a powerful sense of responsibility in the perpetuation of a sacred art. "But you heard it," he says. "It's still alive!"

NY PHILHARMONIC OPEN REHEARSAL

Avery Fisher Hall, 10 Lincoln Plaza
- www.nyphil.org/ConcertsTickets/season/open-rehearsals
- 212.875.5656
- See website for schedule
- Admission: $17
- Transport: 1 train/66 St – Lincoln Center

I hate seeing men in tuxedos

You don't need the spiel about how great the New York Philharmonic is. You know it's great. If you like great music, you should see a concert here. There's more than one way. "I hate seeing men in tuxedos," says C.J. Miles, who waits in the ticket line. "It makes *me* uncomfortable." That's why he's come to Avery Fisher Hall in the morning to hear Dmitri Shostakovich's *Eleventh Symphony* a day before the actual concert. This is the open rehearsal, and it attracts various types: tuxedophobes like Miles, but also people like the friend next to him. "You will hear," he says, "a day earlier than opening night, almost an identical concert. But here's the main difference," holding out his just-bought ticket, thumb pressed firmly on the price: $17. It's half what you pay for the worst seats on a normal night.

Miles, it turns out, is a percussionist who is no stranger to orchestras; for him, a black tie or gown no longer has the otherworldly glow. If you don't mind your artists looking like actual people, there's a reward in seeing a crowd in jeans and tee-shirts attack their instruments to build a great brilliant beast of breathtaking sound around them.

And at a rehearsal you learn about process. Conductor Semyon Bychkov walks in like a sparring boxer with a towel over his shoulder; he drapes it over a chair in front of the podium and unpacks his baton, which is kept, like a tiny instrument, in a special rectangular case. The rehearsal is a straight run-through; then an assistant, who has been following along in the lower seats with a fat score on his lap, points out moments that could use more attention. This is where the orchestra is revealed as the organic machine that it is. Bychkov isolates the brass section for a couple of bars, adjusting the intensity; then the rest of the orchestra joins in for a test run. Better. "OK," he says, "45 to 47, once," attacking a transition where a giant swell falls off suddenly to a tonal whisper. He raises the baton—and it's wonderfully startling to hear the group break into mid-cataclysm from a dead stop. "Thank you, everyone!" Bychkov says at the end. The orchestra applauds; those in the string section with a violin in one hand and a bow in the other stomp their feet. The conductor buries his face in his towel and heads back to wherever conductors go when the music stops.

MONDAY NIGHT MAGIC

The Players Theatre, 115 Macdougal Street
• www.mondaynightmagic.com
• 212.615.6432
• Shows every Monday night except major holidays
• Tickets: $37
• Transport: A, B, C, D, E, F and M trains/West 4 St; 1 train/Christopher St – Sheridan Sq

A jam session for magicians

"**O**ften the hardest part is not doing the magic," says a young performer in the lobby, "but making people care." It could be the motto of Monday Night Magic. The show was founded in 1997 when Michael Chaut and his business partner Peter Samelson, both professional magicians, felt the need for a venue where illusionists could perform regularly. At the time NYC magic was in a slump, and without the amazement of a public, the craft simply dies. "When musicians jam," says Chaut, "they don't need an audience. When magicians jam, they do. Monday Night Magic is this sort of eclectic bunch that just love the art of magic, and the audience is invited to this secret session. We don't advertise—it's all word of mouth."

Now the show, after changing theaters a couple of times, has settled comfortably into Macdougal Street and dazzles week after week like a law of nature. You'll find tourists and locals, pros and amateurs, but with a performing guild that's based on secret tricks, there's a strong unity among the in-crowd. You sense that the friendly lady who shows you to your seat might, on another night, be onstage getting sawn in half.

Chaut says that it's harder to perform in New York than anywhere in the world—harder, if you like, to make people care. Magic has a birthday-clown stigma: amazing isn't enough. What fills the gap is performance style: the magicians here are hilarious, often taking a barbed approach that mocks the old-fashioned image of a gallant sorcerer in tails and top hat. "Coooome to meeee," moans R.J. Lewis, gesturing at a woman from the audience, "coooome to meee." As she struggles to get to the aisle he drops the accent and snaps: "Get up here, honey." By the end, fountains of playing cards are pouring from his open mouth, but if the tricks work, it's the attitude that sells them. Michel DuBois ("you may have seen him on David Letterman") juggles three balls, then five, then seven, and escapes from a straightjacket from atop a unicycle, all while maintaining an edgy patter. Mentalist John Stetson has a teasingly royal, feline approach, pretending to command secret energies through a pointedly campy crystal ball. And his set is flabbergasting. "When you go home," he intones, "tell them 'John Stetson was in my head. *And I liked it!*'"

AMERICAN LEGION POST 398

248 West 132nd Street
- www.colchasyoungharlempost398.com
- 212.283.9701
- Admission: free; two-drink minimum at tables
- Live jazz on Sunday evenings
- Transport: 2 and 3 trains/135 St; A, B, C and D trains/125 St

A beacon for down-to-earth jazz

Among the rows of brownstones on West 132nd Street, there is one with a permanent American flag hanging over the front door: number 248, or officially US American Legion Post 398. The Legion takes charge of veterans' affairs in the neighborhood, and if you're one of the enrolled members, you'll have reason enough to go there. What makes the brownstone a destination for the rest of us is evident if you walk by on a Sunday night, when the sidewalk trembles with muted music. The post has become a beacon for down-to-earth jazz; the attitude, given the history of the spot and its nature as a tribute to military veterans, has an old-school appeal, an aura that is loose but gentlemanly. PULL UP YOUR PANTS, reads the sign on the street-level door, OR STAY OUT! Push through into a brilliant howl of jazz.

An 8-foot ceiling, a dozen tables with plastic covers and folding chairs, a bar in the far corner, and a kitchen in the back. Cases of bottled beer are stacked against the wall next to an overloaded coat rack. There is some memorabilia on the wall, but if you need frills, best move along. The fare is fried chicken and greens; now and then the cook, wagging his head to the music, will saunter out in a hairnet and plastic gloves to deliver a meal or collect a plate; because you have to shout to be heard, to ask if you want to order anything he's as likely to just raise his eyebrows and point at his face. The clientele: everyone.

"Over the years," says Seleno Clarke, who heads the Harlem Groove Band, "we have *escalated*, and *elevated*, to diversity. It's what I wanted when I started doing this." Clarke has been playing Post 398 for fifteen years; the band itself is an ethnic map of New York. They have their reasons for playing the regular Sunday gig. "A lot of the music in the city doesn't have a lot of natural soul," says drummer Sean Cameron. "You come in here, you can feel it." Guitarist Tim Ling agrees. "This band's all about the groove," he says. "The most important thing is connecting with the audience." At the end of the first set, tenor saxophonist Paul Valera does this physically, roaming among the tables to shining faces and whoops of encouragement. Between sets, the band is fronted by local singers who deliver jazz standards, melodies that have echoed in this neighborhood for decades.

CLASSIC ALBUM SUNDAYS

• Various venues in New York City, check website:
www.classicalbumsundays.com
• Adults only
• Admission: generally $10

> *Listen to an album on the best hi-fi setup available*

Classic Album Sundays began in the living room of storied DJ and music producer Colleen "Cosmo" Murphy. "People would come over for Sunday lunch," she says, "and I'd ask what album do you want to listen to? And it would sound so different for them on my system—they loved it." What started as lunch has become a kind of global event. In Tokyo, Portland, London, and New York, people come together regularly for an hour or so to listen to an album—one album, from start to finish—on the best hi-fi setup available.

The experience comes naturally with a dusting of devotional zeal. At a Brooklyn club for a recent twentieth-anniversary listening of A Tribe Called Quest's legendary *Midnight Marauders*, presenter Jay Weinstein explains the appeal of an analog LP over digital. "It's actually physical," he says. "It's a needle on vinyl. You get all of the history. You get the pops and the scratches: it's a totally different experience." Past albums include Led Zeppelin *Houses of the Holy*, Jimi Hendrix Experience *Electric Ladyland*, Pink Floyd *Wish You Were Here*. For livelier albums, you might get more stirrings in the listening crowd, but often it's what Weinstein calls "audio yoga"—a stillness that verges on awkward. "But after a few minutes, there's this relaxing," he says. "All of a sudden you're sharing something with people you don't know." One of the perks of Classic Album Sundays in New York is the proximity of the industry; before *Midnight Marauders* begins, DJ and columnist at the hip-hop magazine *XXL* Jeff "Chairman" Mao glosses the 1993 LP's place in recording history, and relays a personal anecdote: Quest member Q-Tip made a secret dub of the freshly recorded album and he and Mao listened to it all that night, the only people in the world who could. "That's my special connection," he says.

"The albums that stand the test of time," says Murphy, "they don't come out of nowhere. There's always a story behind them." This is as good a definition of "classic" as you'll get. As the needle hits its groove and *Midnight Marauders* begins thumping with a level of bass that rattles the skeleton, listeners nod, and mouth the lyrics, and dance in place, and even gab a little at the bar. Weinstein ducks over to the turntable and seats himself between two speakers, head back and legs splayed, lolling there in a vinyl bliss.

JUDD HOUSE

101 Spring Street
• www.juddfountation.org/new-york
• 212.219.2747
• Transport: N and R trains/Prince St; 6 train/Spring St; B, D, F and M trains/Broadway – Lafayette St

> **The art is one with the architecture**

When sculptor Donald Judd bought the five-story building on the corner of Spring and Mercer Streets, the neighborhood was called the Cast-Iron District: the name SoHo, with its whiff of paint-spattered bohemia, hadn't even been coined yet. In this, as in many respects, Judd was a step ahead. A supremely successful artist, he also appears to have been a great success at living. Regardless of how you find his work, you'll likely come away from a visit to the recently opened Judd House with admiration for an individual who determined, in strange and fine detail, the space he called home.

Judd bought the whole building in 1968 for $68,000, which wouldn't buy a cupboard in Hell's Kitchen today. The move was apace with the artist's expanding dream: he had just won a Guggenheim fellowship, had large sculptural work on the brain, and a family to look after. But his wife Julie Finch called living there "camping out:" there was no electricity at the beginning, the furnace was busted, the many windows let in the winter cold and amplified the summer heat. The building was steeped in sewing-machine oil from its days as a sweat shop: it literally oozed out of the walls. But the house is better than beautiful or cozy (although now it's both): it reflects a mind. With its tidy collection of works, it also expresses Judd's philosophy of exhibition. "Most artists," says guide Stacy Seiler, "they rented. Judd was lucky enough to own his own home. And you'll see that there are no pedestals here: the art is one with the architecture. He wanted this space to be one experience."

To its credit, the tour avoids sanctimony around a man who seemed troubled by any angle that wasn't precisely ninety degrees. Judd didn't like to be called a Minimalist, or even a sculptor, rather "someone who makes specific objects." The specificity engulfed the maker: there's no trace of a human hand in his work, it's what would happen if plexiglas and steel naturally liked to arrange themselves in forms based on the square. Better than seeing the art is seeing a strong personality in full force: the breakfast table with its rules for the children (plates were allowed, but the ugly milk jug was banished to the floor), the precision-fitted wood furniture, the simple desk where Judd, standing, would draw his comforting boxes for hours.

ESCAPE

FOSSILS AT FAR ROCKAWAY

Far Rockaway Beach, Queens
• Transport: A train to Broad Channel and then shuttle train

> *A real piece of prehistoric New York City*

There are secrets out in New York City's ocean: ancient coastlines eroding into the current. Once in a while fossils get washed up onto the beach, and if you know what to look for, they're basically yours for the taking.

Your guide to this is museum paleontologist Carl Mehling. Mehling has made a career out of being smart and curious; he's a scientist in every sense, but with a touch of the adventurer and a face—beard, scar—that would be at home in a lineup of lobster fishermen. He's the first and likely the only person to have logged fossil finds in every borough, Manhattan included. His secret: he's insane. He really wants to find mineralized dead things, and won't take but-this-is-a-metropolis for an answer.

"What you look for are blobs of gray sandstone with shells embedded in them," he says, picking along the beach at a stoop. "Kind of what you'd picture a fossil to look like anyway." The best time to hunt is after storms: they rattle the deep and make a convenient spread of what would otherwise stay out there. Today the beach is littered with the haul of last week's hurricane, a debris field of driftwood, bottles, toys, the skulls of giant fish, and whole carpets of shells that clunk and crunch underfoot. When he finds a bone, Mehling taps it on his teeth; if it's mineralized (and presumably old), it will make a clink. "This is a little mammal femur," he says, turning a small black bone in his fingers. "Or I guess even potentially a bird," he chuckles. "That shows what I know."

After no more than an hour, Mehling spots a jagged lump half buried in the sand. It's an accumulation of four or five oyster shells welded together by coarse gray rock. "*Crassostrea*, I think is the genus," he says, brushing off the sand. "This is from out there," waving the fossil out at a now-calm sea. "That's what we wanted." How old? Roughly ten thousand years. Not exactly a dinosaur, but the oysters were happily going about their business of being alive long before humans had writing, or large-scale agriculture, or cities.

EXPLORERS CLUB LECTURES

46 East 70th Street
- See website for lecture schedule: www.explorers.org
- 212.628.8383
- Transport: 4 and 6 trains/68 St – Hunter College

> *Adventure headquarters*

New York City may be the world's most regular arrangement of concrete, glass, and steel, but it's also home to a few people whose idea of normalcy includes, say, knowing how to swing a machete or build an emergency snow shelter. The Explorers Club on the Upper East Side is the headquarters of the type, and also attracts adventurers from the wider world. The place emanates virile energy in a somewhat bygone style: past members peer from the framed photos with defiant eyes; the wood paneling seems to breathe an air of pipe smoke, tropical sweat, and frostbite. Impossible decoration is in harmony here: a pair of snowshoes, an airplane propeller, an elephant tusk. Learn more and you'll be staggered by the depth of history on offer. That weathered globe is the one Thor Heyerdahl used to plan his epic voyage on the raft *Kon-Tiki*. Those sleds hauled Robert Peary to the North Pole.

To become a member you have to apply: it helps to have done something amazing. But on Monday evenings the club opens its doors to the meek public for a lecture. Cave-divers, climate scientists, astronauts, wilderness experts: this is where the daring come to share what they've learned about Planet Earth. Recently adventure journalist Peter Potterfield spoke on the greatest hiking in the world; when he mentions the name of the seasickness drug he took during the harrowing boat ride to Antarctica, one or two attendees can be seen quietly recording the name in their notebooks. (Just in case: meclizine.) "You can walk for days," Potterfield says of Arctic Sweden, "and never run out of space." This line sends a palpable shiver of desire through the audience.

"We get people who have been to bizarre places," says Robert Ashton, one of the lecture organizers, "tops of mountains or bottoms of oceans. Or who've escaped this or that." (Ashton's own feat: sailing the world nonstop for a decade.) He points out the brightly colored flags that line the walls, some of which have been on several noteworthy expeditions. But the best thing you get out of an Explorers Club lecture might be what you hear in the library over drinks. "There's so many interesting stories that the members can tell you," says club officer Will Roseman (bush pilot in Africa). "It's just awe-inspiring. To me, that's what makes the club alive."

CANOEING THE BRONX RIVER

May to September
• Check website for schedule: www.bronxriver.org
• The Bronx River Alliance hosts free paddles during the summer as well as paid and private excursions

> *A watery dream in the middle of the borough*

The Bronx River, narrow, calm, and only 24 miles long, runs down the middle of the borough. You can step out of the striped shadows of the roaring elevated train, walk just 100 yards of asphalt and concrete, and come upon a fluvial dream: wooded banks hopping with whitetail rabbits, an air aflutter with birds, and the slow water slipping south under the hanging branches of ancient trees. Once you've witnessed this, you'll find yourself struggling to convince other New Yorkers that it exists. The river, named after Jonas Bronck, who built a life in the area during the earliest days of Dutch settlement, in turn lent its name to the whole borough. It touches the city's historic core, and while you'll be content to walk the banks, the best way to see it is floating in a canoe.

"It's not *exactly* like it was," says Linda Cox, executive director of the Bronx River Alliance, which has committed itself to the river's appreciation. "It was straightened in places, mostly for the trains." If this is a defect, it's being gradually corrected as shoring efforts give the stream what Cox calls "natural sinuosity." While you're paddling lazily under a slowly advancing canopy of willow and oak, and see turtles and darting minnows in the shallows, you won't be annoyed that things aren't curvy enough: you'll be too busy redefining an entire metropolis. "People who discover the Bronx River," Cox agrees, "start to see the city differently."

The Alliance offers various canoeing trips, some of them free to the public and confined to one area of the river, others for a small fee that will get your pioneering blood up: long descents through the woods, and then industrial flats, and eventually out into the Long Island Sound. As is true for virtually every organization that seeks to revitalize interest in the city's nature, the Alliance has had a positive impact on wildlife. "We're like the *capital* of that," says Cox. A few years ago a bizarre animal waddled into these waters and found it good: a beaver. The last ones to make a home in the Bronx River died two centuries ago, wiped out by the fur trade that was the basis for the city's very foundation. Asked if she gets more satisfaction from people discovering the river by canoe or the rebounding nature, Cox says, "Luckily, I don't have to choose! You can have both."

FISHING OFF SHEEPSHEAD BAY

- www.seaqueenvii.com
- 917.643.0265
- Fee: $35
- Half-day excursions at 7 am, 1 pm, and 7 pm
- Transport: B and Q trains/Sheepshead Bay

Before you start stepping into the street and methodically knocking people's hats off, get to the sea. It's easier than you think: at Sheepshead Bay, the inlet where Coney Island meets Brooklyn, the sea actually comes to meet you halfway. For the price of a couple of movies, you can step onto a boat and thrum out into the wide waters of the Lower Bay with a baited pole in your hand, angling for monsters.

Get to the sea

"My biggest fish ever," says Randy, "was this striped bass." Randy has a tattoo of a weeping Jesus across his back, with the motto "In Memory of MOM" underneath; on his shoulder another tattoo depicts a fanged clown leering through shreds of skin. Like all the experienced guys, he stays at the back of the boat and keeps, in his smartphone, snapshots of his greatest catches. The striped bass is about the size of your average preschooler. "But today we're fishing for fluke. Hmm," circling his puckered lips with a savoring gesture, "that's the best meat!"

If hooking dinner out of the ocean isn't enough to set your mind straight, take in the sight of terns and gulls drafting behind the boat in hypnotic patterns, or the faraway waterfront where the Cyclone, Parachute Drop, and Wonder Wheel of Coney rise in pale silhouette like the remnants of a long-gone world. When somebody gets a bite, the whole deck springs into action. "Leave it in the water!" yells one of the staff to an open-mouthed teenage girl whose pole has suddenly gone nuts, "I'll get a net under it!" And he wrestles the fish from the line, stuns it with a karate chop to the head, and throws it in a bucket. "There you go, Melanie!"

Every half-hour the captain squawks over a loudspeaker: "OK, guys, lines up." The engines cough into action and the boat heads off into fresh waters. "In some places it's only 10 feet," says Steve, whose tattoos are Irish-themed. He detaches a clump of mussels from his hook with disgust. Then recasts, holding the tip of his pole down near the lapping water, one finger laid gently across the line. A few minutes later he comes up with a baby sand shark. "Nobody's gonna beat him," he grunts, referring to Randy. "That's it, I'm done." And he leans over with his lighted cigarette to burn the bait and hook from his line. As the boat heads back to the bay, Randy collects the pot for biggest catch ($150 for a 27-inch fluke) and leaves a healthy tip for the deck hands. "Every day I don't have work," he says, "I come here. They treat you right."

DOG WALKING AT BARC

253 Wythe Avenue, Brooklyn
- www.barcshelter.org
- 718.486.7489
- Adoption hours: Tuesday to Saturday 12 – 4 pm
- Volunteer walking hours: these vary, see website
- Important: always call ahead

*Make
a break
from the shelter*

This one's simple. Head over to BARC in Williamsburg, and break a dog out of the clink for a couple of hours. It's miles more than just fun. You'll feel roundly rewarded, a little like Robin Hood: rebellious and good at the same time.

BARC is the strained acronym of the Brooklyn Animal Resource Coalition, a non-profit shelter for dogs and cats. If you're a cat person, there's a second floor on site—the mostly scary-sounding "Cat Loft"—that teems with them, and where a certain type can volunteer as a snuggler. Robert, the laid-back manager and adoption overseer, has figured this out. "You think about it: dog people are more, like, outdoor people," he says. "Cats are nocturnal, in a room, sits there, ignores you. There are certain people that like that."

People that don't like that can sign up for volunteer walking hours and make a dog practically expire from joy. When they're not out, BARC's dogs, most of which were saved from a summary death sentence at the city pound, live in wire runs. If you're thinking about adopting, Robert will take you for a tour of these runs; otherwise a random dog will be brought out to you on a leash. The reason: when a person enters, the place goes nuts. It's audition time. There are pure breeds here, and many mutts from puppies to adults, but all the dogs know one thing: outside is better. And strangely, among these wagging, barking, pawing jumpers, one will stand out. Your dog. Robert has placed more than 1,000 in homes, but some just never get a break. "We have a no-kill policy," he says. "So some of these dogs, they've been here for years. That one—"pointing to an ancient chow-chow panting in a funk of medication—"he's 15, 16. Nobody's going to adopt him." A lifer, in other words.

If you've never walked a dog in the city, you'll quickly learn what you've suspected: there's an entire culture for it, with a host of rules and customs. The other dog folk will exchange looks and greetings with you. You will become instantly more interesting to everyone else. You're no longer some random person pacing the hard city, with a loner's problems and anxieties. Now you're on a team.

SOLSTICE YOGA IN TIMES SQUARE

- www.timessquarenyc.org
- 212.768.1560
- Admission: free
- Held June 21: reservation required to participate
- Transport: N, Q, R, 7 and S trains/Times Sq

Mind over madness

I f like many you're not totally sure what yoga is good for, and also can't remember what or when the summer solstice is, there is a peculiar event for your convenience. For the last dozen years on June 21, the spandexed masses have gathered to practice their usually private and inward-looking exercises in the honky, sultry, dirty, neoned jukebox of Mammon that is Times Square. The tradition started with just a handful of inspired devotees who glimpsed, among the heaving tourists, a hint of the eternal sublime: there is a flood of unharnessed forces in that place. Why not use it?

"A broad welcome," says one of the planners into a microphone, "on this, the longest day of the year, a day when the sun is delivering more energy to us than on any other." The sun right now is perceptible only as a bright strip of sky high above the gully of convulsing advertisements, but the point is interesting. Can loose energy be assimilated? If so, Times Square does in fact make an ideal spot. And if popularity is any indication, it works: the ground is carpeted with stretching bodies, each one on a branded yoga mat. "We think it's grown," says the loudspeaker, "because it really taps into what all of us are really trying to do, which is: engage with life."

Serene professionals lead the sequences of poses, also via microphone, so although the four or five massive groups crammed behind barriers from 42nd Street to Duffy Square move in unison, their guidance is a gentle, disembodied echo, as invisible as Vishnu. "Close your eyes just for a moment," says the voice, "and just feel whatever you feel …" This is a tall order with oglers and photographers at the barricades, and the nine trillion pulsing watts, and the endless human spectacle: an illegal Ecuadorian dressed as the Statue of Liberty, an Iron Man that is one part plastic helmet and nine parts dirty pajamas, cop cars, guys hawking comedy tickets. "Feel yourself touching the earth …" says the voice, where the earth is painted asphalt, vibrating to Midtown traffic, and dotted with cigarette butts and pigeon shit. But this is the point. Stay long enough, and follow the motions of these concentrating thousands, and soak in the context and the chaos, and you might detect an inner buzz as a titanic current—the essence of New York—juices you up.

> During the summer Bryant Park holds regular group yoga sessions on the lawn. Check website: www.bryantpark.org

SEE A YANKEES GAME ... ON STATEN ISLAND

Richmond County Bank Ballpark
75 Richmond Terrace, Staten Island
• www.siyanks.com
• Playing season April – September; see website for game schedule
• Transport: a five-minute walk from Staten Island Ferry
• Tickets: $10 (basic seating)

Minor
pleasures

Minor League baseball doesn't sparkle with half the glitz of the majors, but the toned-down vibe has its own appeal. There are really two battles playing out on the ball field: the contest between vying teams, and each player's personal struggle to move up to the big leagues. The fans, who are relaxed but sincere, see the path from Staten Island's tidy little stadium to the hallowed behemoth that houses the "real" Yankees in the Bronx as a smooth continuum. When you root for this team, you root for a dream of success.

"This is our club," says a woman wearing a glittering getup on the Yankees theme: sequined cap with the club logo, spotless Yankees shoes, and a tailored jersey with Mickey Mantle's name and number on the back. "It's the minor-minor-leagues," she admits, "but this is where we get our up-and-coming players." Her husband leans his mustache into the conversation: "And the other park? Forget that crap. By the time you get to the Bronx, you're *shot*." The minors are important enough to draw, albeit compulsively, the madmen who slouch in the section behind home plate and scribble down the stats. "I guess it's all right," says one of these human computers between batters, "if, you know, there's no majors league games happening. I do numbers at the office all day," he says, "and then at night I do numbers at the ballparks." With a haunted smile he returns to the columns and figures on his dog-eared notebook.

The ballpark designers, proud of you for making the sea passage over from what Staten Islanders call "New York," have ensured that everything else is easy. The park, a few steps from the ferry landing, is clean and inviting; when the sun goes down and the sky becomes the strange stadium cerulean behind dazzling field lights and the players jog out in their bright uniforms, it's as though the sport of baseball was freshly minted. This is also the ball field with the best view in the world. Out beyond the crisp greens and painted lines, the shoulders of Manhattan skyscrapers rise in pale silhouette like benign monitors, while ferries continually come and go in the Upper Bay. "A Yankee's a Yankee," says Rudy, a local fan with a coke in one hand and two foiled hotdogs in the other. "At the other stadium you're looking at a *train station*. Here we got all that—" motioning to the skyline. "This is *inspiration*."

MOSHOLU-PELHAM GREENWAY

Begins near the Canine Court on the west side of Van Cortlandt Park (at about the level of West 253rd Street)
• Detailed map at:
http://www.nycbikemaps.com/maps/bronx-bike-map/

> *From woods to beach: the whole borough by bike*

New Yorkers who have never been to the Bronx assume that it's a concrete waste carpeted with discarded drug paraphernalia and dotted by fire; others know that it has more greenspace than any other borough in the city. It's possible to see a fair amount of that green—as well as lakes, rivers, estuaries and open sea—by hitting the largest parks, strung one after the other on a continuous bike path. And "bike path" doesn't mean a painted lane between a sidewalk and roaring traffic, strewn with dangers: it means you cross the borough nearly from end to end on your own strip, without ever having to share the road with a car. There are hundreds of miles of ambitious bikeways proposed in the city: this one, the Mosholu-Pelham Greenway, is ready for you.

The path is marked by colored oval blazes—and you'll need them, because Gotham doesn't give up this much smooth biking without a fight. In Van Cortlandt Park, the trail wanders into others that cross the forests and fields there; at the lake a man with gold teeth and a fishing pole ("largemouth bass," he says, "and yellow perch") points in a direction that turns out to be correct, but only after crossing through a patch of cattails. Once you get clear and begin rolling south, though, you'll know that you've struck on a great thing. The path even performs a corkscrew to keep you clear of the concrete overpasses that hum with traffic as they cross the park—a hum that, since it has no impact on your comfort, sounds almost interesting. In one or two places you need to cross a street, but often enough the light is green and you fly through: the city is on your side.

There are places, as at the beginning of the bumpy stretch along Pelham Parkway, where it seems that your charmed trail will peter out into a mess of urbanity—and then you veer into a shadow and under rows of tall gingko trees. And the blazes aren't always exactly clear, but puzzling out the path adds a dash of challenge. There is a way to cross the Bronx on a bike. You will find it.

By the end you're at Orchard Beach; you started at a wooded lake, and now you're looking at gulls drifting over Long Island Sound. There's even another gold-toothed fisherman here, of a different sort: a guy with a metal detector and a perforated scoop. "I find rings," he says, "sometimes. It's like I says: people at the beach, they lose things." He shrugs and moves on.

SANDY HOOK

Direct ferries leave from Pier 11 and Pier 35 in Manhattan, generally May to October
- Two services:
Seastreak: www.seastreak.com, 800.262.8743
NY Waterway: www.nywaterway.com, 800.533.3779
- Fee: varies, about $40

> *The wild entrance to the Lower Bay*

The first time Europeans entered the waters where the Hudson River flows into the Atlantic was 1524: the Italian explorer Giovanni da Verrazzano and his crew. Verrazzano described "a very pleasant situation among some high hills through which a very deep river deep at its mouth forces its way to the sea." "Pleasant" was a bit of an understatement: the explorer had discovered the best natural harbor on the planet. Look at a map of New York's Lower Bay and you'll see the Rockaway peninsula of Queens on one side, and on the other a mirrored peninsula, Sandy Hook. The two suggest, strikingly, matched doors opening inward to welcome Atlantic travelers into the inner calms, and further up to a merchant's dream of tranquil berth: Manhattan. Everything that made New York possible flows from this fortuitous arrangement of land and sea.

Sandy Hook is in New Jersey, but to appreciate how perfectly and securely New York City lies at the mouth of the Hudson, you can't do better than make the trip out to the peninsula. Ferries leave from piers on the east side of Manhattan; during the trip, which is 45 minutes long, you pass from skyscrapers to industrial lowlands, under famous bridges and out to the river mouth, where you dock at a curl of land where sunflower and cactus grow.

At the landing is a sign: "Take your trash with you when you leave." Lower down, lettered by hand, is the warning "HIDE YOUR FOOD" next to a cartoon of a seedy-looking raccoon. You can camp on Sandy Hook from May to October, and it's one of the few places with a clear view of the city where you can make a legal fire on a beach. A slow-talking ranger leans on the sign, welcoming New Yorkers onto this patch of wild. "People don't even realize that this park exists," he says. "They're, like, from a concrete jungle. This out here is paradise."

The sand is strangely coarse, full of clamshells and busted crabs, and there are nests among the grasses, deepening the general feeling that the place is better suited to contemplatives than the Frisbee–radio–sunscreen set. Grey-headed fishermen, well into their store of beer, sit heavy in beach chairs and talk, with a view of a tiny, faded, snug Manhattan in the distance. Asked if he's had a bite yet, one throws his hands up and pouts his mustache as if to say: "Who cares?"

SHOREWALKERS

• Walks cover all five boroughs and beyond; see website for calendar: www.shorewalkers.org
• Fee: free

> *Seeing the world at 3 miles per hour*

If you've heard of the group of New York foot explorers who call themselves Shorewalkers (motto: "Seeing the World at 3 Miles per Hour") it's likely for the Great Saunter, a creeping marathon held every May that hugs the waterfront for a complete circuit of Manhattan. That's 32 miles. "You have the *option* to walk all the way around," says an older gentleman who wears a button on his chest with the slogan "Polite New Yorker." "We had a thousand people last time, and five hundred finished!" He feigns dejection: "I'm not among them." Many of the other regular hikes mix topography with feats of endurance: try the Great Manhattan Bridge Walk, where you cross all of the island's walkable bridges on a twelve-hour slog. Others are relative strolls: straight down Ocean Parkway from Prospect Park all the way to Coney Island, or today's walk of 5 miles from Bay Ridge to Sunset Park in southern Brooklyn.

"The longest I did was from Inwood to the Battery," says Cheryl, a regular. Not shabby: it's the entire length of Manhattan. "It was painful. But what fascinates me about these walks, is I see neighborhoods that I wouldn't normally go to." Often the territory covered has no conspicuous appeal, and slyly reversing your assumptions may be the best thing Shorewalkers offers. "You'll turn a corner," says Cheryl, "and all of a sudden you'll have an unbelievable view."

Walk enough and you might begin to suspect that nothing is boring—an awesome state of mind. In Bay Ridge you tramp down to the Beltway to a sight of the Verrazano Bridge that verges on the mystical. Further north is the virtually unknown Narrows Botanical Garden. "It's the largest community garden in New York," says landscaper Jimmy Johnson, taking a break to share the spot he's devoted himself to. "We've got ponds, streams. There's a pollinating garden over there where we keep the beehives." Further on you see a monument to the Viking Leif Ericson (it's just below the Valhalla Playground: Sunset Park was once heavily Scandinavian), and walk up through New York's second-largest Chinese population, passing along the way an old cinema converted into a Turkish mosque. You can see all this by yourself, but you likely wouldn't go as far. "The next day, you're paralyzed," says group leader Bob Lazaro of the longer, heroic walks. "You gotta go with somebody. A companion to talk to. That's why we do it."

MOSES MOUNTAIN

Greenbelt Park
- www.nycgovparks.org/park-features/virtual-tours/greenbelt/moses-mountain
- 718.667.2165
- Trailheads, maps, and parking at High Rock Park at the end of Nevada Avenue, Staten Island

> **A one-of-a-kind view and a slap in the face**

As noted elsewhere (see page 203), Greenbelt Park running through the middle of Staten Island is one of the city's great unsung wonders. The natural beauty there is so impressive, it was deemed worth ruining by the greatest and worst parks commissioner in New York history: Robert Moses. Moses was as single-minded as an evil robot. His answer to the urban planning riddle: rip it up and lay a clean, wide strip of asphalt over it. He came close to wrecking the Greenbelt, and the park's highest point, Moses Mountain, is both a reminder and a back-handed tribute. This hill is entirely composed of the rubble left over from Moses's aborted plan for a cross-Staten Island parkway.

It wasn't the only time a Moses project was thwarted by citizens who saw a future mazed with car traffic as less than ideal. The commissioner's plans to expand a parking lot along Central Park and run a sunken boulevard through Washington Square and the West Village were defeated; the Greenbelt protest was helped by a nudge from State Governor Nelson Rockefeller. By the time the Greenbelt section of the parkway was abandoned in the late 60s, rock had been blasted, roads dug up, houses razed. The earth and debris hauled off to this location, eventually topping out at 260 feet, still has the feel of unfinished business, even though the whole mess has gradually turned as green as Peru. As you climb up, you can see crags of old asphalt jutting from the dirt, and the cement pipes of uprooted sewers.

But the real wonder of Moses Mountain is the view out when you've scrambled up to the summit. It's here that the tease in the name people have given this spot is keenest. Instead of an endless chain of cars creeping through the forest, you see gulls wheel lazily over an unbroken landscape of billowing emerald. It's the kind of view that's missing nothing, but would look very nice with, here and there, the long bowing neck of a grazing dinosaur. It's the only place in all of New York City where you can stand at the top of a landmass and see a horizon that is nothing but trees.

QUINTESSENTIAL NYC

METROPOLITAN CHAMPIONSHIP ㉑

Gleason's Gym
77 Front Street, Brooklyn
• www.gleasonsgym.net
• 718.797.2872
• Admission: $20
• The Metropolitan Tournament is held in the late fall
• Transport: 2 and 3 trains/Clark St; A and C trains/High St; F train/York St

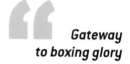

*Gateway
to boxing glory*

Gleason's Gym, Brooklyn's temple of pugilism, offers dozens of events during the year. It's the home of White Collar Boxing, where amateurs are given a venue to beat the hell out of each other in front of a crowd; it has weathered the shift of the neighborhood to higher-rent with strenuously hybrid programs like *Strike!* ("boxing/chamber music/dance concert"). But if you want the purest dose of the blood–sweat–tears potion that transforms the sport into a metaphor for personal struggle, come watch the Metropolitan Tournament.

The guys call it "The Metro." It's the last major hurdle before the country's most elite contest, the Golden Gloves, and the fighters, many as young as 15, rightly see it as a gateway with a vision of glory shimmering on the other side. The youths radiate a unique vibe: swaggering, methodical, nervous. Each is looking to improve his "book," the record of wins and losses that will decide a career. Once in a while a brawler will come off the street with enough raw talent to make a mark quick. "That's what you look for," says Elmo, a trainer. "They're the ones that bring the excitement." More often it comes down to sweat. A Rockaway boxer, swinging his fists as he awaits his turn at the physical check, agrees. "You could be talented," he says, "but a person who works hard will beat you any day. *Any day.*" These are some of the most disciplined teenagers you will ever meet.

Show up before the bouts start and you can follow the personal stories: the background narrative that will culminate in a crash of guts and strength in the ring. "I'm two–three," says Jonathan, shadow boxing with fresh white tape on his hands. That's two wins, three defeats. A look of controlled worry passes over his face. "Wait, no: two–four." Another fighter sits on the edge of the ring, already gloved up, spitting on the floor with studied nonchalance. George, just 15 and a first-timer at the tournament, sulks back from the weigh-in to his trainer. "I'm a pound and a half over," he says. The trainer hands him a jump rope. "You got fifteen minutes. Lose it." Asked if a person can really shed a pound and a half in fifteen minutes, the trainer shrugs: "Yeah," with the unspoken note that it depends on how much you want to. In the end George doesn't. Glory packs up her laurels and leaves quietly out the back door.

MANHATTAN
LIVE **CHICKEN**
VIVO **MARKET**
987-2099
248 E. 117 ST.

HALAL
VIVO
248 E. 117 ST.

INS Manhattan
Live Poultry
HALLAL-VIVERO 212-987-2099

VIVERO: LIVE POULTRY MARKET ⓻²

N & S Manhattan Live Poultry
248 East 117th Street
• 212.987.2099
• Open every day 8 am – 6 pm
• Transport: 6 train/116th St

> *For some,
> fresh is better*

A *vivero* is a shop that sells animals, generally poultry, and then kills and guts them for you. There are a few in New York; the one on 117th Street in Spanish Harlem has a neighborhoodly air that makes it worth visiting even if bird is off the menu. Buyers make a selection from the stacks of squawking cages, and then wait in a line that is the NYC working-class immigrant experience in concentrate form. Chinese, South American, Mexican, West African, Caribbean—you can find anybody. The management is Arab (many *viveros* slaughter according to the halal strictures of Islam). "The whole United Nations comes here," summarizes Charlie, a Puerto Rican who keeps a small fruit stand at the entrance. What the customers share is a yen for freshness, and an unsentimental approach to meat. A man eating a salami sandwich can paint himself a misty picture of the life of the pig; here you look dinner in the eye. In the kitchen when you pull the carcass from the bag, it's still warm.

"Fresh is better," says Rogelio (Mexico) and next to him his wife nods enthusiastically. They buy a chicken a week, mostly for soups. Fresh is not pretty, though. *Viveros* have stacks of steel cages crammed with birds: entire walls of rustling plumage and gloomy stares, bathed in the wan glow of fluorescents. The stink is eye-watering. But the shop fascinates. If you've ever eaten a commercial chicken, this was its life. The men who come and go in plastic aprons—the men who bind and weigh and cut the chickens with mechanical efficiency—they're clearly beyond caring. But if you've never seen such a place, you'll sting from your brush with mortality. Eating is killing, it's hard to get around it. A *vivero* in the Bronx has a sign on the wall: "Goat head: $5." Under it a dozen goats munch placidly at a bale of hay.

While you'd never confuse a *vivero* with a pet store, there's nothing to prevent you from buying a live chicken and taking it back to your studio apartment for a steady diet of corn chips and HBO. In fact, some customers buy live animals, but for a fate many would call worse than soup. Followers of Santería, the Christian–voodoo mashup brought to the city by Caribbean immigrants, need birds and goats for ritual blood sacrifices and *viveros* are generally where they get them. But then, nobody said New York was boring.

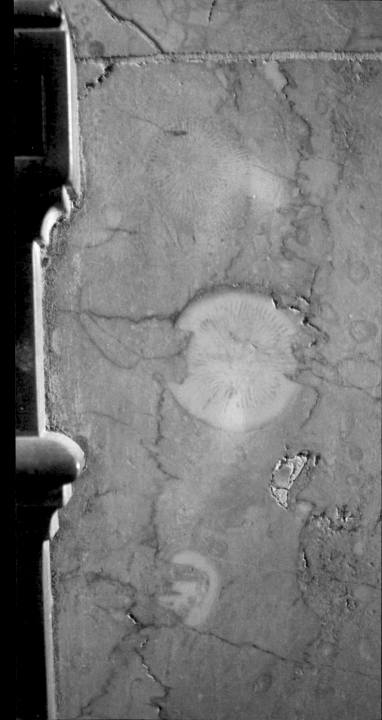

URBAN FOSSILS

Ancient beasts in the walls

New York City is a prime spot for fossils. The Museum of Natural History has one of the largest collections on the planet. If the wild calls, you can pick up your own fossil in the hurricane debris of the city's beaches (see page 143). There is a third, perfectly metropolitan way to connect with the deepest kind of history: hunting for the long-dead animals frozen in the quarried stone of buildings. Nobody had these accidental exhibits in mind during construction. It gives architectural fossils a special appeal: the building is just a public surface until you arrive, with your squint and your curiosity, and make it a museum.

TIFFANY'S

The red limestone that surrounds the display windows is full of ancient sea lilies, plant-like animals related to the starfish. Studying architectural rock brings home how the city has collected material from all over the globe: this stone formed around 100 million years ago, in what would become Spain.

SAKS FIFTH AVENUE

The stone of the cornices has the toothsome name "Ste. Genevieve golden vein marble" but it comes from Missouri. It's dotted with Devonian corals (pictured) that lived 360 million years ago.

MACY'S

The pillars of the lower floor are dressed with a stone similar to the one above; the best fossils are in the handbag department. The impressionable lady next to you is thinking about dropping a thousand perfectly good dollars on a Louis Vuitton; you are examining sea creatures that lived before the earth had land animals, or leaves, or insects.

ROCKEFELLER CENTER

Perhaps the most surprising display of fossils. The dun Indiana limestone that faces the entire surface of the towering G.E. Building, as well as every other building in the complex, has been kept appealingly rough: you can still see the drag and blade marks from the quarry. At two paces, it's just rock. Lean in and you'll discover a fine tapestry composed of the remains of tiny creatures: hundreds of different species that settled at the bottom of a tropical sea that once covered the Midwest. (The same rock faces the Empire State Building and the Metropolitan Museum of Art.)

BASE OF CLEOPATRA'S NEEDLE, CENTRAL PARK

American Museum of Natural History geologist Sidney Horenstein, whose fascinating work is the basis of this entry, has called the white limestone under the Egyptian obelisk "solid fossil." Every bit of it is shot through with the disk shells of nummulites (the name comes from the Latin for "coin"). There's a thematic connection: it's the same stuff the pyramids at Giza are made from.

STORYTELLING IN CENTRAL PARK

On the west side of the Conservatory Water at about East 74th Street
• Saturdays 11 am –12 pm June to September
• Admission: free
• Transport: 6 train/77 St; B and C trains/72 St (walk through the park)

> *Once upon a time for half a century*

You can walk by the large bronze statue of Hans Christian Andersen in Central Park without suspecting that you've just passed the city's premiere venue for storytelling. The statue of the author of *The Ugly Duckling* (and *The Little Mermaid, The Princess and the Pea, The Emperor's New Clothes* …) was designed as inspirational backdrop for those who would carry on his art, regularly, in this place. It's a tradition that goes back nearly sixty years. The founder of what is officially called the Hans Christian Andersen Storytelling Center was one Baroness Alma Dahlerup—who sounds like she escaped from her own fairytale—and her bona fides as an Andersen proponent were ironclad: she heard his tales directly as a child, sitting on the writer's knee in their native Denmark.

Where the park setup isn't quite so intimate—the storytellers use a microphone and the seats are arranged concert-style in rows—it has going for it a sterling setting. The statue's base becomes a stage for tales, shaded by the branches of a great oak, backdropped by redbud and squirrels, and looking out over the sailboats crossing the pond. And the storytellers here are some of the city's best. When LuAnn Adams gets up to deliver *The Teapot*, she colors Hans Christian Andersen with brassy, emotional voices that quaver and hiss and roar, depending on the character and moment. "Once there was a teapot who was *very, very proud*," emphasizing the word "proud" so much that it comes out in a deep growl.

This is riveting stuff if you're a kid. Or if you've entered the kid's natural territory of narrative bliss. It's interesting to turn away from the stage, and monitor its power. On a summer weekend the park is full of people; as they

pass the statue many of them glance, and then slow their pace, then stop—and fold their arms, hooked. The children sit with mouths open and eyes focused on the storyteller but seeing distant places: drunk on tales.

CITY HALL LIBRARY

31 Chambers Street, Room 112
• www.nyc.gov/html/records/html/library/chlibrary.shtml
• 212.504.4115
• Open Monday to Thursday 9 am – 4:30 pm; Fridays 9 am – 1 pm
• Transport: 4, 5, 6, N and R trains/City Hall; J train/1, 2, 3, A, and C trains/
Chambers St

A hidden library, open to the public

The Surrogate's Courthouse on Chambers Street has the extravagant beauty that the law in its grander moods likes to project. The entrance is vaulted in the city's best mosaics; an inner courtyard is clad in a warm stone that suggests fine leather, just one of a few unusual marbles here. Too bad almost no one goes in. Visitors in general don't know about the building, and those who do are put off by the security. They're all missing out on a treasure: a handsome public library located on the north end where New York keeps countless documents about the city's favorite subject: itself.

"I think our important mission is to make it more accessible," says Alexandra Hilton, the young librarian who directs the visitors center. "We have so many resources that people don't know about." The archives range from documents that could involve you personally—like birth, death, and marriage certificates—to the minutiae of the city's offices and services, which furnish the library (by law) with copies of whatever they publish. The records room (go past the armchairs and the grated fireplace) has proceedings, reports, and budgets from every imaginable department; browse the shelves for five minutes and you'll be struck by the fact that New York is imponderably vast, and it saves everything, and it's all kept here—for you. A steel vertical file has a drawer labeled "Vandalism." Open it, pull the file, and discover that in 1954, the apes in the Central Park Zoo were given prototype swings to see how they'd hold up to savage abuse, "on the theory that youngsters with vandalism in their hearts are no more heavy-handed than carefree gorillas." There's even a picture.

The library has a trove of biographical material on city mayors going back to the 1600s. "LaGuardia kept a lot of stuff," says Hilton, "and he would write back to every single person." In the municipal archives reference room, you'll find the microfilm roll "LaGuardia: Curiosities–Maniacs." Insert the film, whizz it to the index number, and read a letter to the mayor from a young lady in Edinburgh which begins: "I'm writing to ask you if you know of any nice man (with money) who would like or who wants to meet and marry a nice, smart, very good-looking English girl." "There's a whole file labeled 'Lonely Hearts'," says Hilton. "Some of them are sad, and some of them are just ridiculous." They're also local history in a finer grain than you'll get anywhere else.

WOOLWORTH BUILDING LOBBY TOUR

233 Broadway
• www.woolworthtours.com
• Check website for schedule
• Transport: 2 and 3 trains/Park Pl; E train/World Trade Center; N and R trains/City Hall; A and C trains/Chambers St

> **New York's most beautiful lobby**

For over a century, the lobby of the Woolworth Building has been generally considered the city's most beautiful, a legendary status deepened by a decades-long policy of keeping people out. At the entrance there's a sign: TOURISTS ARE NOT PERMITTED BEYOND THIS POINT—which is annoying, because beyond that point you can spy a tantalizing glimmer. Those who ignore the sign and march freely through the doors (the building houses offices) take on an air of mysterious privilege. Finally, you can join them: in 2013 the Woolworth celebrated its centennial, and for the first time since World War II, average folk have been invited to enter and gorge their eyes during regular tours led by a knowledgeable staff.

Once the tallest inhabited structure in the world, the Woolworth was the culmination of the dawn of the skyscraper in the early 1900s; New York then paused as though to take a breath before the so-called skyscraper races of the late twenties gave us our classic titans. While the Empire State and the Chrysler look forward, stylistically, the Woolworth is born from an odd mix of conservative and lunatic: it takes medieval Europe and stretches it out to fifty-seven floors. But admirers of the cool Gothic steeple, capped in verdigris, might be surprised that the interior radiates exotic: rich Byzantine. The mix is a one-off. "This space could never be created today," says guide Jason Crowley as he leads the group up the regal central stair. "There was an abundance of immigrant labor here, and you can see the incredible level of skill," pointing out a carved stone belt course where each vertical is decorated with a unique human face. "Everything here, down to the doorknobs, was individually designed."

The glass mosaic tile ceiling ("the crown jewel of the lobby") is the source of the formerly forbidden glimmer you saw from the sidewalk, but these individual carvings looking down on you are far more interesting. Famously, the key players in the Woolworth's construction are depicted in the entrance hall, each figure bearing the emblem of his profession. The chief engineer has a truss; architect Cass Gilbert holds a scale model of the building you stand in; Frank W. Woolworth himself, who began his career as commercial emperor in the humble stock room of a general store, carefully counts stacks of coins. A plain-dealing man, Woolworth paid for his astonishing building—all $13.5 million worth—in cash.

SOCIETY OF ILLUSTRATORS

128 East 63rd Street
• www.societyillustrators.org
• 212.838.2560
• Sketch night Tuesdays and Thursdays ($15); check website for many other events
• Transport: F train/Lexington Av – 63 St

> *It's still about the visual impact*

I n the stairwell of the Society of Illustrators hangs a painting by the legendary N.C. Wyeth: a young couple in medieval dress backed up against a tree and staring out at an unknown threat, crossbow cocked and loaded. It sums up the illustrator's art: the painting is beautifully observed, with surprising colors and subtleties that fill the scene while keeping your eye on the action—but the image is unfinished. At the top there's a blank banner where, down the production line, someone would print the title of a book (*The Black Arrow* by Robert Louis Stevenson). Illustration is not art for art's sake: it's art for *your* sake, to help you visualize a precise message. For the people who make it, the Society is home.

"This place is Mecca," says Gregory Manchess. "And it's been that way for over a hundred years." Manchess is a painter, and the third-floor "Hall of Fame" dining room is currently filled with his work. It's vivid stuff: yelling pirates, loping dinosaurs, explorers with polar bears for pack animals, muscled barbarians swinging axes. There's adventure and mystery, saturated skies and gorgeous flames. Manchess has attained the highest level in the art, but remembers visiting the Society when he was just starting out. "Every time I'd come in here I'd get goosebumps," he says. "I learned a ton."

You can, too. Aside from galleries showing works from a large private collection and revolving exhibitions of prominent working artists, and an

entire floor dedicated to the Museum of Comic and Cartoon Art ("the world's most popular art form"), the site also offers direct experience: twice a week the dining-room tables are cleared and anyone interested can come and add their easel to the dozens set up around a live model. When you become a big shot, the Society will be your clubhouse. Expect solid people. "The thing with illustration," says Manchess, "is it's still about the visual impact. It's still about storytelling. It's not just about the ideas, it's about pulling it off altogether." In other words, it's refreshingly bullshit-free. And as such, an antidote to the mediocre mirror-gazing that often fills the other kind of contemporary art museum. You know: high art.

CIRCLE MANHATTAN WITH THE AIA

Classic Harbor Line
• www.sail-nyc.com
• Tour leaves from Chelsea Piers
• Fee: $76

> *Architectural perspective*

Manhattan—this island crammed with buildings—is too big to fully contemplate when you're in it. No doubt there's a large enough percentage of the population that lives there or travels there daily by train more or less happily for months at a time without ever getting a glimpse of a river. But out on the water is where your perspective lies. "There are walking tours," says Doug Fox. "And you can take a special architecture tour. But to completely circle Manhattan in three hours and see how it has changed through the years—you can only do that from a boat." Fox is one of a couple of members of the American Institute of Architects who lead the tours offered by Harbor Lines, transforming a pleasure cruise into an education. It's whatever the opposite of rubbernecking is. On a recent voyage most of the people who bought tickets, and attached themselves to the rail to gaze at the smoothly passing profile of Metropolis, were New Yorkers.

The commuter yacht leaves from Chelsea Piers, itself a lesson in the shifting forces of the New York City waterfront. The piers once serviced a harbor of bustling docks and gangplanks and machines—some of which endure as relics—for lading ships. When river trade faded, the piers were left to rot; now, within a wider theme of sprucing up the town, it's an enormous sports complex. The yacht berths behind this; step aboard, take a seat, and try to understand this behemoth of a city.

As you head up the Hudson, generalities become clear. The almost futuristic dominance of the freshly minted Freedom Tower, the Empire State's noble loneliness, the sudden wild of Riverside Park at about 72nd Street, where residential towers give way to forest. You observe particulars, the details of balconies, window surrounds, and decoration that reveal a governing style or architectural firm's trademark. You learn how the city works, for example the reason behind the most distinctive element on the New York skyline, the water towers (a reserve is necessary because the system loses pressure after the fifth floor). If nothing else, the trip is a comprehensive lesson in city bridges from a vantage that reveals how they were made, and how they work: the swing bridge at Spuyten Duyvil that alternates between ship and train traffic, the Triborough's vertical lift.

NEWTOWN CREEK
WASTEWATER TREATMENT PLANT

329 Greenpoint Avenue, Brooklyn
• www.nyc.gov/html/dep/hmtl/environmental_education/newtown_
wwtp.shtml
• 718.595.5140
• To schedule a tour, send an email to: educationoffice@dep.nyc.gov
• Admission: free
• Transport: G train/Greenpoint Av; 7 train/Vernon Blvd – Jackson Av

*I lost
my ring! Help!*

You've likely already seen the Newtown Creek plant at some point, if not while traveling through the city at least on a screen: the facility, a collection of thirteen-story stainless steel orbs that shine with reflections all day and glow lightning-bolt blue all night, is a favorite of TV and movie location scouts. It looks like a titanic machine installed by aliens bent on readying New York's atmosphere for a future invasion. Actually, pretty humble science is used here to remove and clean the water from crap. Your crap.

Once a month, Newtown offers a tour which begins with an in-depth presentation from an engineer. Many of the attendees are hard urban planning types themselves, and the specific questions they ask will open the door on a world of activity that you've taken for granted all these years. People devote their entire lives to making cities run smoothly. The art of great infrastructure is going unnoticed: you flush the toilet, and forget. After the flush is where Newtown gets to work.

The tour covers every stage. You see the boilers and the huge pipes and conduits, and you visit the electrical control room, which looks exactly as you're imagining, and you learn that Newtown does its best to be a good neighbor: odor is surprisingly under control. In fact the only space that really smells like anything is where machines rake the muck from the primary filters, and then splat the muck onto a steel chute. The fumes here, if abruptly more pungent, are not overpowering, something like the cage of the world's most slovenly hamster. Asked what interesting things have been caught in the screens over the years, the plant's superintendent Jim Pynn first freezes the group's blood with horrors, then adds: "But sometimes you get a five-dollar bill coming through. People call and say: 'I lost my ring! Help me!' We try. And you know, sometimes we've been successful."

An elevator takes you to the gangways at the top of the mysterious orbs. The boilers you saw earlier are devoted to heating them to the exact temperature of a human gut, because the action here—bacteria breaking down matter at a rate of 3 million gallons of goop per day—can be seen as an extension of your own organism. The orbs are properly called digester eggs, and digest is what they do. Then the resulting "sludge cake" gets barged upriver and packed off to a farm. You know: circle of life.

TENEMENT MUSEUM
"EXPLORING 97 ORCHARD STREET" TOUR

103 Orchard Street
- www.tenement.org
- 212.982.8420
- Admission: adults $25, children, students and seniors $20
- Exclusive evening program; check website for availability
- Transport: F train/Delancey St; J and M trains/Essex St

*Inside
the walls*

Poor people generally don't leave much of a mark on history: it's the big shots who erect the fancy buildings and monuments. The Tenement Museum on the Lower East Side sweeps this tradition aside by preserving an entire building—97 Orchard Street—that housed over 7,000 residents during a career that began in 1863. These were ordinary folk, poor folk: laborers and immigrants from twenty different countries who weren't much distinguished beyond the fact that they helped seed an entire nation. "Historians say that one in six Americans can trace their ancestry here to the Lower East Side," says the museum's Kira Garcia, "because these tenements were so densely populated, and because this was the first stop." We can imagine easily enough the bewildered Irish, Italians, Greeks, and Eastern European Jews who gazed up at the Statue of Liberty from the deck of a steamship, or spelled their exotic names to the staff of Ellis Island, but where did the huddled masses go once they hit New York pavement? They came to a place like this.

On top of a regular program of guided visits, some featuring costumed actors, the museum gives a special evening tour where the broader themes of New York immigration are broached through a level of detail that is practically forensic. The museum began twenty-five years ago, when tenements like this one could be bought fairly cheaply. Instead of going the typical route—gutting and remodeling—the founders made the building an opportunity in urban archaeology. Every inch is loaded: pressed-tin ceilings, papered plaster that has crumbled down to the wallboards, iron-treaded stairs, and generations of paint that has peeled and curled and cracked so thoroughly, some surfaces look more like birch bark than wall. "There are layers and layers and layers," says Garcia. "Of paint, of wallpaper, of linoleum. And each layer is a chapter in the building's history." Each layer has also been studied under a microscope, providing a temporal map: wave upon wave of tenants.

New Yorkers know that the more recently a family has immigrated here, the less likely they are to be excited to talk about it. "Some people see this as really beautiful," says Garcia. "Some people are depressed by it. Old people still remember living in places like this and wanting to get out of them." Any visitor will leave with a vivid impression of what it's like, and what it takes, to stack hope against hard luck and get on with making a life.

GROLIER CLUB EXHIBITIONS

47 East 60th Street
- www.grolierclub.org
- 212.838.6690
- Admission to exhibitions: free
- Transport: 4, 5, 6, N, Q and trains/59 St

> *Your ticket into a private society of book lovers*

The Grolier Club on East 60th Street is a private society established in 1884; it's the sort of place that has its symbol carved in marble above the entrance. The members are connected by a love of fine books (it's in fact the oldest book-appreciation club in the U.S.) and, as you might expect, inside broods a noble and tantalizing library that you, guy or gal off the street, are barred from pawing. "You have to be nominated by a current member," says interim exhibitions coordinator Jennifer Sheehan: "collectors, librarians, staff members at institutions of note … that kind of thing."

The club's foundational constitution outlines a mission to foster the love of books and works on paper principally through the library, but also through publications, the maintenance of the club building as a resource, and exhibitions. These last have been, for 125 years, the average New Yorker's ticket inside. At an impressive pace of ten shows a year, the Grolier Club makes a gift of fine books and supporting material on a particular theme: woodcuts of the Italian Renaissance, a history of snake oil medicine, polar exploration ("Books on Ice"), Whistler in Venice.

The hall is only one room, but it's stocked with surprises. In the recent exhibition "Extraordinary Women in Science & Medicine," you learn that the first person to introduce advanced mathematics in Italy was the philosopher Maria Gaetana Agnesi—who, by the way, had learned seven languages before she was a teen. It's one thing to know this; it's another to see a 1784 copy of her pioneering *Instituzioni Analitiche* on display. Florence Nightingale, already distinguished enough for her hospital work, was also a groundbreaker in statistics and information graphics: her clear, beautiful, and strikingly modern "Diagram of the Causes of Mortality in the Army in the East" from 1858 hangs on the wall. An area devoted to Marie Curie offers books and manuscripts, but also an original apparatus she used in her earliest work on radioactivity. "You can see these dark spots on the wood," says Sheehan. "When it was delivered they told me it was originally a somewhat different color, but when they found out it was radioactive, they went in and tried to sand off the varnish." If you know that the brilliant Curie later died from a disease connected to radiation exposure, this simple wood-and-brass contraption seems to fairly hum with significance.

SCICAFÉ AT THE MUSEUM

American Museum of Natural History
Central Park Week at 79th Street; SciCafé entrance on 77th Street
• www.amnh.org/learn-teach/adults/scicafe
• 212.313.7278
• Admission: free
• Held the first Wednesday of the month; see website for event details
• Transport: B and C trains/81 St – Museum of Natural History; 1 train/79 St

A lecture, and a bar

I f you've ever sat before your booze and thought: *You know what's missing from this? A scientific journal* (or vice versa), the Museum of Natural History has a regular event for you and like-minded people. The SciCafé, held on the first Wednesday of the month, features a lecture from a prominent researcher, and a bar. That's really all you need to know. It's a socially safe environment for really smart adults, perhaps the only one in the city where "What's your favorite star?" is a more likely pickup line than "What's your sign?"

The topics are sometimes curious, always compelling: how dinosaurs evolved from birds, assessing the livability of planets outside the solar system, whether we will ever be able to grow a wooly mammoth from frozen DNA. In a museum that contains everything, there's a special resonance between the collection—miles of corridors, exhibits, and storage stretching all around—and the specialties of the invited speakers. On a recent evening Dan Lieberman, chair of human evolutionary biology at Harvard University and famous proponent of barefoot running, discussed how modern society can benefit from recognizing our paleolithic roots; to summon our species' development he had only to mention "downstairs," where the whole story, from lemurs through Lucy to something like you, is neatly laid out. And without leaving the building, one could go further: where mammals came from in the first place, and what cultures modern man built for himself. Every province of science touches others, and testing and enhancing that web of information is the central aim of a SciCafé speaker's career—and about as much as you could expect from a night out.

While Lieberman speaks about how you evolved to want things like Pop Tarts and shoes and smart phones, but not need them, you can scan the listening audience at their tables, in candlelight, with the neck of a stuffed dinosaur curving above them. "It's a baby Barosaurus," says one man afterward (of course, somebody knows). The crowd is a nice blend, though: in one circle of folks discussing the talk there are a scientist, a physician, a woman who works in PR, and a boxer/substance-abuse mentor. "I thought a lot of his points on epidemiology were pretty much on-point," says the physician. "But I disagree," says the boxer, "with the idea that infectious disease is no longer a big issue." "Oh, so do I, completely." Guys, get a room.

NATURE

BRYANT PARK BIRDING

www.bryantpark.org
- 212.768.4242
- Spring to fall; see website for schedule
- Admission: free
- Transport: B, D, F and M trains/42 St – Bryant Park; 1, 2 and 3, N, Q and R trains/Times Sq

> *Nature in Metropolis*

A bird migrating over the island of Manhattan cruises on a frigid tailwind at over 100 miles an hour, 1,000 feet up. Down below appears an inviting rectangle of green. Bugs, seeds, and rest wait down there. When you stroll in a city park and see a modest thresher pecking at the lawn, you're crossing the path of a great traveler, and strangely Bryant Park, a swath of lawn girt by towers of glass and steel, is a place to do it. Through the Audubon Society, the park offers birding tours from spring to fall, and while there are fewer species here than in Central Park, Bryant offers the starkest collision of Nature and Metropolis you'll find anywhere. And surprises abound.

"Is that a woodcock?" asks Vinnie, a birder from Brooklyn. "It is!" He's pointing in the direction of the carousel, and the group—about half a dozen—turn their binoculars in unison. There, blinking shyly, is a creature few people have ever seen in the city. The woodcock has curious eyes: they're set so far back on the head, the bird has depth perception behind, where danger lurks, but not in front. The feathers form broken jags and dashes, a camouflage that works as well in the leafy flowerbeds of Bryant Park as in woodland. "I can't see it," says one woman, squinting at the leaves. The Audubon guide, Gabriel Willow, knows how to handle this. "Do you see that bench?" he asks. Nod. "Do you see that rock to the right under the bench?" Nod. "OK, that's the bird." The woman's jaw drops.

Willow is an urban ecologist (see page 197), and his take on birding, and city living in general, can hardly be improved. "One of the beauties of being out in nature and exploring birds is it can take you out of your own city concerns sometimes, and transport you a bit into their world. You're in a little reverie, watching the woodcock rooting around for worms or something, and it's really interesting, trying to think how they experience this landscape. We saw half a dozen people go by that woodcock, totally oblivious, walking to work. And if they were aware, how might it make their day a little more interesting to see this incredibly improbable bird?"

You can see around 280 bird species on the island of Manhattan; about 200 have been spotted in Bryant Park.

FORAGING IN CENTRAL PARK

- www.wildmanstevebrill.com
- 914.835.2153
- Suggested admission: $20
- Transport: B and C trains/72 St

> *Meeting plants on their own terms*

Central Park is edible. If you take the tour led by "Wildman" Steve Brill, this unexpected truth will be proven in minutes. "Kousa dogwood," he says before a decorative tree near the West 72nd Street entrance. "They planted it because it has lovely white flowers in the spring." It also has bumpy fruits of an intense vermilion; Brill immediately splits one open and devours the pulp. He appears to remain alive. Encouraged, others in the group pluck their own, clambering around the guy who sells John Lennon buttons next to the water fountain. The peddler is used to this: "I think the birds got most of them," he says, squinting into the tree. Brill sings back: "That's because they bought my app!"

Brill is an institution: tours, classes, apps, books. His niche is urban foraging, and the nickname "Wildman" has all the burlesque you'd expect from a guy who speaks with a Queens accent and wears a safari hat in the middle of America's most unnatural city. But this is the core of the tour's appeal: eating Central Park seems like a trespass of order. And the safari hat actually serves: a few paces from the dogwood, Brill grasps a hawthorn branch and yanks. "That's why I wear it!" he says as a rain of small fruits thuds onto his head.

Tiny hawthorn fruits, it turns out, taste like apple, and virtually every one has a nodding worm inside. "It's actually not a worm," Brill happily explains, "it's a maggot." But sooner maggots than pesticides. It's a theme: nature is better left solving its own problems. Foraging is a form of exploration, of meeting plants on their terms, and it doesn't matter if they grow in the shadow of skyscrapers. If you want wax polish, go back to the supermarket. "Quickweed," Brill says of a low ground plant with sawtooth leaves. "First I tried it raw, and it tasted like a hairy leaf. Then I cooked it, and it tasted like a cooked hairy leaf." (The secret: make a purée, add it to soup.)

Among the plants that humans can eat, there is no single unifying feature but rather a balance of two: the presence of nutrients, and the absence of poisons. Brill can tell you what's what, and share a few tricks. Yellow woodsorrel is as citrusy as lemon. Epazote weed is good for hangover. Sassafras smells like root beer, and tingles on the tongue like chewing gum.

BAT WALK

Central Park
• Check website for schedule: www.nycaudubon.org

The night shift in Central Park

At dusk Central Park becomes a different place. The racket hushes, the trees darken against the graying sky, and the fragrances of flowers and earth grow more intense. The air is richer, sweeter. "All the bushes and trees are breathing now," says naturalist Gabriel Willow (see page 193). He has led a group into a clearing in the Ramble encircled by tall sweetgum and oak. "They don't do it like we do—they sort of take one long breath all day, and then exhale oxygen in the evening before they go to sleep. It makes it feel good to be out." That trees might sleep (they close tiny pores in their leaves) is just one of the evening's surprises; another stirs on a branch high overhead: a bushy gray raccoon. "Just waking up," says Willow, "he's got to go to work raiding trashcans." And on cue, the nocturnal raccoon slowly clambers down the trunk in what really seems to be a grumbly, blue-collar manner. Suddenly the main attraction flits high in the sky overhead: an erratic shadow against the dim sky. "You see!" says Willow. It's a red bat on the hunt.

There are five species of bat in Central Park, and they rule the night. They have no natural predators because nothing flies well enough to catch them. And the agility of bats is coupled with what seems to us a superpower: the ability to "see" in the dark by means of a high-frequency cry. Humans can't hear it, but Willow now pulls from his backpack a small black box that can bring the sound down to our perception, with a dial for varying the sensitivity. He knows the red bat's range—he knows a million curious things—and as the green digital number nears 38 kHz, suddenly the box makes an unearthly chitter of rapid clicks. As another red bat cuts a curve above the trees, Willow follows its course with the gadget, and this ordinarily hidden dimension—a hunting bat's night vision—becomes bizarrely audible. Unlike birdsong, it's not a call: there's no message. It's a sonic paint that bats spray onto the world around them, providing a resolution so fine they can discern shapes as thin as a human hair.

These are facts worth knowing. There's a glowing metropolis all around, and when you're out in it, it's good to remember that you might just as easily be strolling in the wooded dark, breathing an air heavy with oxygen and aroma, watching the secret habits of night-shift animals getting to work.

WILD CHICKENS IN THE BRONX

Corner of Edward L. Grant Highway and 169th Street, Bronx
• Transport: 4 train/167 St or 179 St; B and D trains/167 St or 170 St

The natural landscape

For the strangest dose of pastoral in the city, head to the Bronx parking garage on the corner of 169th and Edward L. Grant Highway. For years, wild chickens have lived in an old birch tree that overhangs the sidewalk. The chickens aren't in fact totally wild. They're whatever you call domestic birds that have been left to themselves in a landscape of asphalt and broken glass, bordered on one side by a busy street and on the other by the roars of the elevated train, kept alive by anyone (maybe you) with a giving disposition and a handful of rice.

"*Por la mañana*," says the fruit seller's wife: in the morning, that's the best time to see them. Then they strut in force on the sidewalk. "And in the evening," says Alfredo, a neighborhood Dominican who sits on a beach chair in the parking lot, "right around six, six-thirty"—he flocks his fluttering fingers up over his head—"they go up into the tree!"

This is not a neighborhood much visited by outsiders, so for the most part the passersby ignore the chickens as part of the natural landscape. Many of the kids here no doubt believe that every parking garage in New York City chortles with scratching hens policed by a handsome blond rooster. "It's part of our daily life," says Eddie Guerrero, an attendant at the garage. "We don't give it too much importance, but it makes the day better."

Eddie has a peppery beard and long hair greased back on his head, and wears an Argyle vest and a tie. There's a calm and a directness to him that suggest you've stumbled on the resident guru. "They live up there in that beautiful aspen tree that's been there for many decades," he says. "They sleep there every day, they get out of the tree every day, they take their rice, they eat, they gather, they drink, they clean their feathers. It's a good thing these animals live among us, because they're beautiful, and they respond to nature."

The chickens roost up in the old tree not because they have a sense of urban poetry, or a sense of urban anything: it's just good old-fashioned staying alive. "They gotta protect themselves from raccoons and rats," says Eddie. Raccoons eat chicken? "Oh," he widens his eyes, "a raccoon will tear a chicken up." Now you know.

SOLAR OBSERVING

Central Park, at the Conservatory Water (east side at roughly 74th Street)
• Observing scheduled once a month; check the Amateur Astronomy Association website: www.aaa.org

Astronomy at noon

What does the sun actually look like behind the dazzle? Not too many people know first-hand. You can be one of them: once a month, the Amateur Astronomy Association reverses the classic image of a star-gazer—a dedicated loner peering into the infinite black while the rest of the world sleeps—by setting up a public observation station at noon in the middle of Central Park. Nighttime astronomy you can do with or without a telescope, although never very well in New York City: a wash of artificial light dims the distant stars and planets. The sun is the opposite. There's too much of it.

"It's a unique look that you obviously don't get in ordinary life," says Tom Haeberle, the Association treasurer. He squints into a small telescope on a tripod, gently edging the front lens over midtown, right into the brilliant eye of a clear winter day. The telescope is of the normal optical variety, but outfitted with filters that block 95 percent of the light. Through it the sun appears as a flat, pale yellow disc almost totally filling the field of view. In an upper quadrant there's a tiny, completely still dark spot—what could be a speck on the lens. It's actually a raging magnetic storm the size of the Earth. "A sunspot is a kind of depression," says Haeberle, "much colder than the photosphere, which is why it looks black." The photosphere is this telescope's specialty, and although strictly speaking the sun has no surface, the photosphere is the next thing: it's where the sunlight we perceive originates.

Alongside this instrument is one with a different trick: a hydrogen alpha telescope. "It blocks out all the visible light," says Haeberle, "all the infrared and ultraviolet, and only a certain sliver of wavelength comes through." This filtering makes visible an outer layer of the sun: it's fierce and red-orange, and the more you look at it, the more detail opens up: the grain, bumpy like a rind, and pockets of relative dimness, and the whole perimeter trembling as if at a low boil. Around the edge also appear the trails and filaments of solar prominences, streamers and strands like halted explosions. It's in part this surface activity that makes our star become mysteriously real, and appear to be, for probably the first time in your life, what it is: an enormous ball.

NEW YORK'S WILDEST PLACE

- www.sigreenbelt.org
- 718.667.2165
- Trailheads, maps, and parking at High Rock Park at the end of Nevada Avenue, Staten Island

Remotely fascinating

I n the hive of Metropolis, there are expanses of wild: great parks, beaches, and lonely urban wastes like abandoned airfields. But there must be a place that is more remote from the buzz of people than any other—New York City's wildest spot. According to one writer (Bruce Kershner), it's on Staten Island. There, in the middle of one of the city's truly great parks, the underappreciated Greenbelt, is a spot that is 1,488 feet from any public street or house. Is this the record? If you accept it as the goal of a day's adventure, you won't care. Inside the Greenbelt, you are gone.

Logical that the wildest spot would be on Staten Island: the place is only partially tamed. Sidewalks tend to disappear in the interior, and the ground cover seems to come in three varieties: mugwort, poison ivy, and another kind of poison ivy you didn't know about yet. The "Forgotten Borough" is fully one-third parkland, and the Greenbelt is the prize. "This is New York City's last self-supporting ecosystem," says Pete Ziegeler, who wears National Park Service green. He trudges around the soppy rim of a pond, ducking under bushes to get an uninterrupted view of the other shore, which, on this golden afternoon, might have been arranged by a sentimental landscape painter. Ziegeler works at nearby Great Kills Park, but when he clocks out he comes here. At another pond, where the swamp trees rise out of the shallows and the water is dimpled by water skippers, a patient researcher takes photos. "It's for a survey of dragonflies," the man says. "So far about twenty-seven different species have been found in this area. Give or take."

To a New Yorker's gridded experience, this might as well be the Russian Taiga. Kingly trees—oak, sweetgum, hickory, beech—permeate a weird terrain, the so-called kettle ponds and bogs that are the legacy of the last ice age. It's within reach of public transportation: the whole trip of subway, ferry, and bus will cost you $2.50. That's a bargain for a trek that starts at a noisy intersection and ends, just a couple of hours later, on a fallen tree over a bog grunting with toads. The wildest spot is on the most easterly bank of Hourglass Pond. You can find it, probably, by using the trail guide and following the blazes on the trees. If you don't, you've still done something that counts as pretty particular.

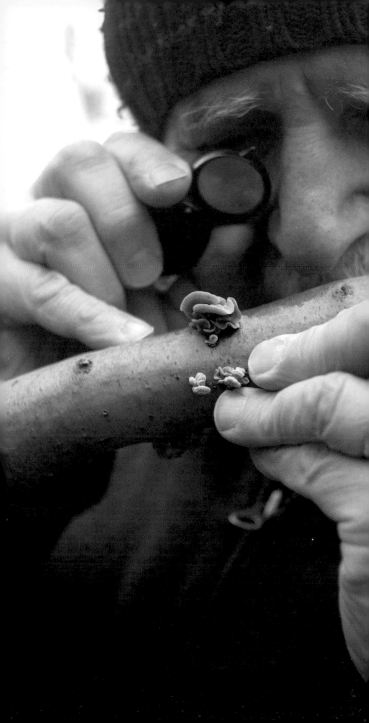

MUSHROOM HUNTING WITH THE MYCOLOGICAL SOCIETY

• Free hunting forays take place in the city parks throughout the year; check Society website for schedule: www.newyorkmyc.org

A deeper, stranger dimension

The New York Mycological Society, officially interested in all things fungal, meets regularly for walks in the city's parks. The unexpected is nearly guaranteed. "There are over 500,000 species of fungus," says professor and crust fungi expert Tom Volk, visiting from Wisconsin for a walk in Inwood Hill. "And that's an estimate. So it's more the rule than the exception that there's something you can't identify."

Fungi are unglamorous, but they're a keystone of a healthy ecology: nature's silent, arcane janitors. They stick close to the soil, and moist crannies, and deadwood. They grow in the dark. Some of them *glow* in the dark. And the people who study them are the sort who value substance over pizzazz, who get a thrill from finding a deeper and stranger dimension in the apparent mundane. Because mushrooms and other fungi are generally small, this deeper dimension becomes dramatically real under a loupe (most of the members wear one around their neck). The surface of *Trametes hirsuta* looks ordinary enough until you peer through the lens—and then suddenly you might be looking at the hide of a silverback gorilla (Latin *hirsuta* means "hairy"). A slime mold's oatmealy texture is actually countless reaching stalks, dispersers of spores that ride on tiny air currents wafting just millimeters above the forest floor. "You find them," says the group leader, the New York Botanical Garden's Gary Lincoff, "and then you identify them. Only later when you learn about them do you understand what they're doing." He's holding a stick speckled with what looks like gunpowder. These are endophytes, guardian angel fungi that secrete a toxin to protect the host from pathogens.

This lure of the mysterious animates the mycologist with a slow burn of excitement. And you'll notice immediately: people deep into mushrooms are smart. "Mushrooms are kind of charismatic when you run across them," says Don, who moments earlier confessed that there's nothing that he likes better than photographing fungus. Another seeker carries a clipboard to log his discoveries; he wears a shearling hunting hat, and has a wispy mustache and blue eyes as pale as an iceberg. "If you don't find something new," he says with an intensity that seems almost startled, "you're not looking hard enough." If you have to belong to a club, it might as well be made up of people who say things like this.

NORTH BROTHER ISLAND AND THE AUDUBON ECOCRUISE

- www.nycaudubon.org/events-a-adventures
- 212.691.7483
- Fee: $30
- Available June to September; other cruises available throughout the year
- Transport to launch at Pier 17: 2 and 3 trains/Fulton St or Wall St

Reclaimed by nature

North Brother is a small island under the Bronx in the upper sprawl of the East River. Once location of the hospital that housed New York's quarantined and incurables, half a century ago it was given over to nature, which wasted no time in taking over. Today North Brother is unvisited, uncontrolled, and shaggy with wild trees. The ruins give the place a forsaken character—but only from a narrow, human perspective. For the city's cormorants, which nest there, it's home. There are three ways you can see this mysterious place. One, be a cormorant. Two, trespass, and exasperate a cormorant. And three, take the excellent EcoCruise hosted by the water taxis, and led by smart people from the Audubon Society.

New York water taxis, never the first conveyance that occurs to visitors or locals, are, aside from a beautiful way to see the city, an ideal way to watch estuarial nature. Which, as it happens, is rife. "Acre for acre," says the guide over a microphone on the upper deck while the boat throbs through the snapping wind upriver, "estuaries are the second richest ecosystems on the planet." (The first: tropical rain forests.) The taxis are catamarans, and so draw hardly any water, allowing the pilot to pull as close as you can get to the city's small islands without a kayak. These wooded humps rise like forgotten realms, and there's a satisfaction in watching the local birds transact the timeless business of fishing and feeding their young, undetected by the swarms of New Yorkers doing *their* business in the bowers of concrete and glass on the shore at either side.

The guide is full of remarkable facts. Cormorants dive as deep as 100 feet in search of fish, which means they can explore the darkest deeps of the East River with ease. Off Mill Island we spot the very symbol of the Audubon Society: the great egret, a frilly bird pushed to near-extinction by, of all things, hat makers: the decorative plumes were once more valuable by ounce than gold. When the taxi nears North Brother, the wind suddenly whips up as the river opens out to Long Island Sound. "This," says the guide, "is what sixty years of unchecked nature looks like." The photos of North Brother when it was still occupied by people show a flat, well-tended expanse of lawn crossed with paths. That civilization might as well have been a thousand years ago: the roofs of ruined buildings are now just visible through a real New York City jungle.

THE LAST SALT MARSH

Inwood Hill Park, northernmost Manhattan
• www.nycgovparks.org/parks/inwoodhillpark
• Transport: A train/Inwood – 207 St; 1 train/215 St

*Primeval
Manhattan*

Study the northernmost tip of Manhattan on a map, and you'll see it's dented by a small inlet. There, within Inwood Hill Park, is the last saltwater marsh left on an island that was once fringed with pretty much nothing but. The marsh is an ecological time capsule tucked away among the last natural scenery on the most rigidly developed spot on earth.

The essence of a tidal salt marsh is change. At high tide the bay is unexceptional: a body of water fringed with grasses and seawalls of split stone. At low tide it reveals a different nature, becoming a glistening mudflat where channels of water snake out toward Spuyten Duyvil. Birds stoop and peck over the mud, leaving tracks of dimples like stitches in fabric as they jab at holes for fiddler crabs and in the shallow pools trembling with mummichogs.

It's not exactly a forgotten oasis. The tide is the globe's clockwork, and the animal life, which has a knack for ignoring development, goes about its timeless pursuits—but the shore has been shaped by modernity, and even if you drift into a vision of the past, the moans of passenger jets high above will reel you back. What the marsh offers is subtle instruction in preservation. On the north shore of the inlet, there's a station where the city park rangers can tell you as much about the tides, plants and animals of the inlet as you care to learn. Ranger Sunny Corrao looks out over the flats on a bright summer day and talks about the marsh's role as a last of its kind. "People who are coming specifically for that know about it," she says. "Others just see it as a peaceful spot."

Although there's still just enough at high tide to row a canoe, the water was deeper in the 1930s when most of Inwood Hill Park was built: the mud is partly sediment laid down over the decades. It's a favorite spot for birders: you can see egrets, great blue herons, plovers, geese, ducks. Once in a while a goose will give a single echoing honk; then all the browsing geese fly away as a sudden team, wingtips slapping the surface. They leave behind an impostor pigeon (the sign: DO NOT FEED THE PIGEONS) to pick among the shore rocks by itself, as at home in a precious salvaged landscape as in a gutter.

VISIT THE ALLEY POND GIANT

East Hampton Boulevard: the trailhead is on the left just before you
cross the Long Island Expressway (heading south)
• Transport: Q30 bus/Horace Harding Exp/E Hampton Blvd

> **New York's
> oldest living thing**

The oldest known living thing in New York City is also the tallest: a tulip tree in eastern Queens. Getting there requires some pluck, and like much of what is striking and natural in the city, the tree seems forgotten, or lost. It grows next to a snarl of expressways in a corner of Alley Pond Park, and if you make the trek to sit for awhile in its speckled shadow you'll hear, beneath the birdsong, a constant background wash of hissing traffic. But the trip is worth it.

This area of Queens will be unrecognizable to most as a part of Gotham. It's a realm of one-story brick houses that all resemble each other, and so make an effort to stand out with some genteel addition: a plastic deer, a chrome banister, concrete lions. Where East Hampton Boulevard crosses the Long Island Expressway there are, to one side, towering traffic signs and retaining walls and a caged overpass. It's the other side you want: a trailhead with thistle, cattails, and butterflies. At first you'll think that you've been lured into a facsimile of nature: the trail is asphalt and all of the green is on the other side of a black chain link fence. But after a few paces the fence ends. To your left is a deep forest. In it are trees that remember Indians.

The Alley Pond Giant stands only 50 yards or so straight in. After passing a runoff of tumbled rock, you'll head through territory in a hurry to get wild. The ground is spongy with leaves and tulip blossoms; rare ferns sprout in curling clusters, and the damp bark slips from fallen branches when you walk on them. There are several immense trees here, but you'll know when you've found New York's tallest. The Alley Pond Giant has its own fence enclosure; next to the hollow bole is a Parks Department sign trimmed in spiderwebs and beetles: "This tuliptree (Liriodendron tulipifera) is the tallest carefully

measured tree in New York City with a height of 133.8 feet. It is also probably the oldest living thing in the City at an estimated age of 400 years or more. This tree is perhaps the last witness to the entire span of the City's history from a tiny Dutch settlement to one of the great metropolises of the world. If we leave it undisturbed, it may live among us for another hundred years or so."

SEINING IN THE EAST RIVER

93

- www.brooklynbridgepark.org/events/public-events/education-environment
- 718.222.9939
- May to September
- Held at the foot of the Manhattan Bridge (Brooklyn Side)
- Transport: F train/York St; A and C trains/High St

Life in the shadow of the bridge

Seining, the research fishing technique used by Brooklyn Bridge Park Conservancy, involves wading out into the waves and dragging shoreward a 20-foot net (a "seine") with very fine mesh. Whatever was minding its natural business out there gets swept up and laid out for review in the shallows on the beach (and later thrown back). The East River, just something to be crossed over or under in a train for most New Yorkers, is an estuary rich with life that outdates us by millions of years. Blue and striped bass, pipe fish, marine snails, crabs, shrimp, eels … "We mark down everything," says Nick, an environmental science student who handles one side of the net, "so we can understand exactly what's in there, per season and per year. It's a great way to monitor the health of the river and instruct the public."

The place to do this is the small inlet where the Manhattan Bridge meets Brooklyn. The place is like a theater, and the show is New York's essential forces: out across the river rises the dramatic skyline, inland is a grassy park bracketed by the relics of the area's historic industry: brick warehouses and factories. A wooden jetty, bristling with rusty nails, makes a rickety reach for the water; on the other side is the eastern stanchion of the titanic bridge: faded blue iron, chains hanging from the underbelly. Pick your way down the granite seawall at low tide and you'll discover a minute sandy beach where, on weekends, you can explore this part of the scene that would otherwise remain mysterious: life down under the river's surface.

The public is heavy on kids, who watch the net come in with excitement spiced with just a hint of nerves: there's no telling what haunts the deep in the shadow of a great bridge. Plastic buckets filled with water are set out for the more interesting creatures; brave kids touch and handle them. "Why isn't it snapping?" asks a boy about a shore crab. "Because it's too small," says marine biologist Nim Lee, talking through a portable mic system so she can be heard above the serial thunder of trains passing overhead. The crab's spindly legs tread air between her fingers as she holds it up for display. "He would love to snap me, but I'm bigger." The boy frowns down at his own hand as if to compare. Later, he whispers confidentially: "A crab can snap your finger *off*." It's what they call starting the conversation.

ASTRONOMY ON THE HIGH LINE

Hosted by the Amateur Astronomers Association
• See website for schedule: www.aaa.org
• Transport: A, C and E trains/14 St

Oh My God, I see Saturn's rings!

Aside from atmosphere and space, when you look up at a night sky there's nothing much between you and the planet Saturn. The gas giant hangs out there, slightly canted, its rings catching the same sunlight that shines onto your breakfast table. You can see the starlike speck of the planet with the naked eye, but to observe its rings—or the craters of the moon, or the oblong disc of Venus—you'll want a telescope. For the last five years, the Amateur Astronomers Association has made one available to the curious public up in everybody's favorite new park, the High Line.

A perch above the street seems the natural place for stargazing, but as a rule Manhattan works against astronomers. "There are a lot darker and better places," says AAA rep Carey Horwitz with a bleak chuckle. "We just do this as an outreach." He squints into the eyepiece of a 900 mm refractor telescope; out over New Jersey there's a thick cloud bank and behind it, hopefully, Venus. Ideal viewing conditions or not, the people clearly want to be reached: behind him a line stretches southward, and as more telescopes are set up along the stretch of elevated track above 14th Street, there's a talkative gathering, a little like the loose crowd that collects in front of a popular nightspot.

Horwitz holds up a tablet device to the sky; on it a celestial mapping app tells him where, if the clouds move on, the sparkling pinpoint of Venus will appear. A few minutes later it does. Emma, a precocious 12-year-old, gets a reverent eyeful as the astronomer explains that the planet has phases. "Does the waxing and waning have any correlation to the waxing and waning of the moon?" she asks. "None whatsoever," says Horwitz with a science man's happy bluntness. "Kids love it," he says later. "Maybe some kid sees something here, and thirty years from now makes a major discovery in the field. Who knows?"

Throughout the evening there are murmurs of wonder from the various telescopes aimed at different points in the sky. The few observable objects out there are certainly spectacle enough. Now and then someone loses it. "Oh My God, I see the rings," says Adam, here on a date with his girlfriend. "I SEE SATURN'S RINGS!" Later he describes the experience in dazed, almost breathless tones. "It's just like the picture, but real. It was shaky a little bit, but as soon as I saw it I thought: I *know* that. I've seen it illustrated in theory but never *real*."

WHALE WATCHING

- www.americanprincesscruises.com
- 718.474.0555
- Fee: $40
- Season: May to October
- Boat leaves from Riis Landing, Queens
- Transport: Q35 bus/Fort Tilden. American Princess also has a ferry service from Manhattan: check website for schedule

Feeding giants

Whatever else you're doing in the city on a weekend from May to October, you're only an hour or so from standing on the deck of a ship, gaping at humpback whales. You do it just off Rockaway: backdropped by a miniature Manhattan rising over the shorefront properties and silver jets constantly ascending from JFK airport, impossibly huge animals frolic and feed. Humpback whales can measure well over 50 feet in length, and their size makes for pretty indifferent eating habits. "They're not like a dolphin that might chase one fish around," says Christopher Spagnoli, the marine biologist on the American Princess whale watching cruise. "That's not energy-efficient." What they do instead is open their maw, angle for bait fish swarming near the surface, and gulp up hundreds of gallons of seawater with spectacular splashes and booms.

"It's food chain, food chain, food chain," says Captain Frank DeSantis, who's been boating these waters for decades. Tracking what the whales eat is the surest strategy to spotting them, and DeSantis, aside from being an expert, also receives updates from locals on shore. The whales ply the area along the southern edge of the peninsula; they feed on bunkers, a pitiable baitfish which is harassed by blues and striped bass into forming swarms that offer some protection against smaller predators, but make tidy morsels for a cruising leviathan. The massings are called bait balls, and you can see them as a patch of disturbance on the surface. "What you look for is *unusual splashes*," says onboard naturalist Catherine Granton, perhaps overestimating the average New Yorker's knowledge of the sea. But once you've seen it there's no mistake: an area a dozen or so feet across begins to flicker, and then boil with activity, with streaks of froth ripping across like lit fuses, and even the glitter of crazed bunker leaping from the water.

The frenzy of a bait ball seems to have been created as a courtesy warning to photographers. After a few seconds of bunker terror, suddenly the boiling patch is reliably upended by the closing trap of a humpback's bizarre mouth. "Classic lunge feed!" Granton cries. As water is forced around the whale's baleen, a kind of lattice screen where you'd expect teeth, sprays jet out on either side. Then the mysterious titan is gone, leaving only a rainbowed mist, and a slick patch on the sea.

HALLETT NATURE SANCTUARY

The piece of land beyond The Pond at the very southern edge of Central Park (about the level of 60th Street)
• The sanctuary is closed to all visitors except for those on special tours; check the Conservancy website: www.centralparknyc.org/visit/tours
• Transport: N Q and R trains/5 Av – 59 St

> *Birds and coyotes*

The Hallett Nature Sanctuary is notable for contradictory distinctions. First, it may be the most-seen and -photographed of any part of Central Park, since it provides a backdrop to The Pond at the romantic southeast corner where many first-time visitors plan their approach from Fifth Avenue. Second, hardly anyone who contemplates or photographs it knows why it's truly special. Countless times you can stand on the shore and look over those picturesque waters at the fallen trees and wild underwood of the other side without asking yourself why you've never seen anyone over there looking back. You never do. Because this patch of land is forbidden to people: it's really the only part of Central Park that pointedly is.

The policy began in 1934, when these 4 acres were given over to the birds, and has since kept the place anonymous. Ask your New Yorker friend to meet you at the Hallett Nature Sanctuary and you'll get a frown in return. The only sign identifying it is on the less-traveled side opposite the stone bridge. Once you know it's forbidden, of course, it becomes seductive. Water splashes at the top of a rock outcrop, overhung by a crooked black cherry tree, where starlings preen and drink. Wagging tendrils of wisteria beckon from over the fence; outside it are asphalt paths, inside are ferns and mushrooms sprouting from logs. No telling what the birds think when they fly freely over into the woods set aside for them.

"A lot of the animal life has pretty much adjusted to this environment," says Mario, a Conservancy gardener. "But nothing's truly wild in the park, you know?" Mario has been tending Hallett for years; today he's ripping out dense clumps of buckthorn, an invasive species that the park tries to control. It's a Tuesday in October, when, for the first time in eighty years, the general public has been invited to enjoy this private realm. There's a pitched view of Central Park South skyscrapers through a screen of trees, but on the ground it feels like countryside. And for the creatures, it might as well be. Remarkably, in 2010 a coyote wandered onto Manhattan from Westchester, and after navigating a teeming metropolis, found its way here to the sanctuary: the only spot in 34 square miles it might feel totally secure. "I would come in here," says Mario, "and see where he was going, follow his footprints in the snow."

INTERNATIONAL

HAND-ROLLED CIGARS

171 West 29th Street
- www.martinezcigars.com
- 212.239.4049
- Open Monday to Friday 7 am – 7 pm, Saturdays 10 am – 6 pm
- Transport: 1, N and R trains/28 St; 2 and 3 trains/34 St – Penn Station

The neighborhood shop

Since 1974, the city's best *tabaqueros* have been elbow-deep in loose leaf tobacco on West 29th Street, rolling cigars by hand. Martinez Cigars uses traditional methods that no one has ever been able to improve on, and if you like a well-made thing, you might like one even more that has been crafted from a single ingredient, in one place.

"It's the neighborhood shop," says owner Jesus Martinez. The sort of person who buys a cigar is likely to take a seat and smoke it, and when you step in the first time, it's hard to tell exactly who works there and who's just hanging out—as good a sign as any of a happy business. "We know a lot of the guys by name. Other guys just come off the street and fit in like they were here forever." Martinez grew up in the shop, under an eternal cloud of aromatic smoke: his immigrant father Don Antonio Martinez, a cigar roller, was founder. The pictures on the walls have the jumbled, unplanned look of a business that has been left to settle into its personality naturally, and the rolling stations of the *tabaqueros* (one of them, Cristian, has been on the job for over thirty years) are the beat-to-hell originals. "When my dad passed away," Martinez says, "we just changed the names on the licenses. Everything else stayed the same."

The tobacco, like the Martinez family, is Dominican. The raw leaf arrives in bales of up to 100 pounds each, and all that's added is uncanny skill. Aside from the easy conversation and no-frills, quality smoke, the best reason to come is to watch these wizards roll. They start with a handful of leaf, and encase it in layers that rapidly merge with perfect geometry: a cylinder of the desired size, rounded at the end. Cigars range from slender $2.50 varieties to large ones that go for $14. But if you want a freak, Martinez can oblige. "They call this the 125," says Will, a slight man with slow eyes and a dapper overcoat. He holds up a monster that he just purchased, a gauge that might be called the Freudian Ironist. Will admits that the cigar turns heads. "I smoke it on the street," he says. "People look, they take pictures." He slips the cigar back into its paper bag. "I tell them to come here."

SUKKOT

Kingston Avenue and Crown Street
- Takes place mid-Tishrei; see calendar: www.hebcal.com
- Transport: 3 train/Kingston Av

> *Dancing deep in Hasidic territory*

Try this: during the week-long holiday of Sukkot, on any night except Shabbat (Friday), take the 3 train to Eastern Parkway and walk down Kingston Avenue. With every step, you're getting deeper into a cryptic world: Hasidic New York, where Jews adhere to ancient customs, governed by seemingly as many rules as there are human activities. Within this rigid structure, it makes good sense that a time is set aside for society to go completely bananas. Sukkot is it.

As you head down the avenue, you'll be aware of a buzz in the street: men in black hats and suits rushing south, teams of kids in identical striped sweaters leaping along the sidewalks while their mothers—hat, dark wig, warning look—bring up the rear. When you hit Carroll Street, it's clear that these Jews are up to something: the trees are swept by the red and blue lights of parked police cars, on a stage bearded men shred klezmer music on electric guitars, and the street has become a barricaded gully, apparently to keep the throng of leaping and twirling men in black from kicking down the storefronts.

Enter this area (men only), and you'll likely get sucked into the current. "Take pictures later," shouts one reveler. "Now is dancing," slapping his sweaty fedora on your correspondent's head and dragging him by it into the melee. The women watch from the sidewalks, outlined by the glow of dime stores and restaurants, many of which will stay open all night. Aside from the archaic screwiness of separated sexes, the feel is small-town county fair: cotton candy, popcorn, canned cola. If there were room for a Tilt-A-Whirl on Kingston, there'd be one.

Lubavitchers reach out, so be prepared to be ogled first (you'll be one of the few non-Hasidic there) and chatted up later. "Chabad Lubavitch's mission is to be a light unto the world," says Nachman, a young married man. "We're trained to interact with people in general." Lubavitchers believe that their Rebbe Menachem Schneerson (who lived only a couple of blocks away) was the Messiah of prophecy, and tend not to keep this info to themselves. This is why you'll get away with crashing the party: the more people, the more light gets spread.

Does the corner of Kingston and Crown—the heart of the storm—have special meaning in the life of Schneerson? "No," says an older man mopping the back of his neck with a handkerchief. "The Rebbe never cared much for dancing." As he gets engulfed in a jostling wave he thrusts out a damp business card: "Email me!"

JAPANESE ZEN TEA CEREMONY

Urasenke Chanoyu
153 East 69th Street
• www.urasenke.org
• 212.988.6161
• Open Tuesday to Friday 9 am – 5 pm
• Fee: $15
• Transport: 6 Train, 68 St – Hunter College

*Details,
details*

Taking part in the Zen tea ceremonies offered to the public at the Urasenke Chanoyu is an entertaining chance to watch New Yorkers—perhaps yourself included—slowly realize that they are bumbling oafs. The gracious instructor, Yoshihiro Terazono, figures it takes "about thirty years" to become a master of the technique; you will be lucky not to die of embarrassment. "This is not a fun time that you have on a Sunday afternoon," Terazono says in kindly tones, "and you talk about your life and the movie you saw or the book you read. This is not even really about enjoying a cup of tea: this is about being with yourself through a cup of tea."

In other words, it's philosophy. Tea in Japan became infused with Zen in the mid-1500s, and with time the ceremony became codified to a degree that can seem borderline demented. For instance tatami, the bamboo mats that carpet the floor, are of regular dimensions: the performer of the tea ceremony calculates where to set a pot or rest a ladle by counting rows of stitches from the edges. The shape of the entire room, in fact, grows from the spacing of these stitches: a Japanese tea house's floor plan is determined by the precise arrangement, with no overlap, of the tatami that fit within it. This detail symbolizes the whole exercise: here, the small things reign. It's a domain frozen by rules.

"Please take a tea biscuit," says Terazono to one of the guests as a kimonoed assistant—angel of elegance—floats over and offers a tray. "No," he corrects with a smile, "not like this"—dangling his fingers in a grabbing gesture; "like this"—holding his hand to the side, balletically arranged. "This"—dropping his fingers again—"is like a bear." The other bears titter warily.

However you withstand the pressures of exacting refinement, you'll have taken part in some of the rarest Japanese culture the city offers. Once you duck through the wood-trimmed passage into the tea area, New York disappears. The children of the Urasenke Chanoyu staff call it the door to Japan.

Every piece of the Urasenke Chanoyu tea rooms was imported from Japan. The center occupies a 19th-century brick carriage house that was once the studio of Color Field painter Mark Rothko. It's where the artist killed himself in 1970.

RUSSIAN & TURKISH BATHS

268 East 10th Street
- www.russianturkishbaths.com
- 212.674.9250
- Transport: L train/1 Av

*It's only
about the heat*

A mong the brick tenements on East 10th Street, there is one that, since 1892, has provided patrons with a secret passage to Hell. This historic Russian bath comes with a dose of opera: the owners are feuding brothers. "A Boris pass can only be used during Boris's shift," says the website, "and a David pass can only be used during David's shift." Mixups are grounds for angry correction. But if grace is not the Russian bath's strength, it's because grace is not needed. You don't come to be coddled. You come for withering heat.

"Do this," says grumpy Boris-or-David, thumbing a sign that says to leave your valuables in a tray; "Don't do this," thumbing another sign warning not to lose your locker key. That's all the instruction a first-timer gets. On the way to the dressing room a muscled man raises his fist and asks: "Platza?" Platza, it turns out, is getting systematically whipped with oak branches (it costs extra), and the whipper is Mokhtar, a Kazakh from Uzbekistan. This is not as weird as things will get.

Shorts and towels are provided: if you can figure out which is the front or back of your trunks, you'll have solved an enduring riddle. But you don't come to the Russian bath for style, either. Step downstairs, where the different rooms are arranged roughly by temperature. First the redwood sauna, which, except for the foresty bouquet, could be Midtown in August. In the aromatherapy room, things ratchet up: you're among an unknowable number of coughing ghosts in the dense white steam; now and then a drop of scalding water taps you on the head. But these are antechambers to the real furnace, the Russian Room.

"People think that you come here, and you relax and hang out," says Max, a bearded Hasid from Brooklyn. An old hand, he wears his locker key around his ankle. "But it's not about that. It's only about the *heat*." Max sits on one of the dark Russian Room's wooden tiers and submits to a wrathful emanation from the corner: there, behind rough stone walls, is a reportedly 20-ton rock that has been more or less on fire since morning. Along the ceiling are craggy girders that support the building above, reinforcing the notion that you have approached the Earth's molten core. "When I'm thinking too much," Max says, "I come here and reset." He lumbers to a brick basin and upends a bucket of water over his red face. "When I walk out I'm a different person."

BLOOD SAUSAGE AT THE ESTONIAN HOUSE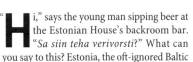

New York Estonian House (*New Yorgi Eesti Haridusselts*)
243 East 34th Street
• Takes place in November; check website for schedule:
www.estonianhousenewyork.com
• 212.684.0336
• Transport: 6 train/33 St

> *Sa siin teha*
> *verivorsti?*

"**H**i," says the young man sipping beer at the Estonian House's backroom bar. "*Sa siin teha verivorsti?*" What can you say to this? Estonia, the oft-ignored Baltic country, has a language more ancient and strange than anything in Europe. "You never know," he shrugs, switching to metropolitan English. "When I come here I try to speak as much of it as possible."

Taivo Ets is a regular at the House, where he sings in the choir, and drinks beer, and eats homey food. Today he's here to help out with one of the most specific cultural events that you might hope to take part in: the making of the seasonal *verivorst*, or blood sausage. The Estonian House was established in a social club in 1929, and among the first to hang out here were sailors in town on a port call. The back room feels cozy, and foreign, and old. Right now it smells delicious: on the tables are tubs heaped with sausage stuffing. "What you're going to see in a minute here," says Ets, "is he's going to bring out vats of blood."

"He" is Siim Vanaselja (all Estonian names have an otherness that borders on intergalactic). Born in the old country, Vanaselja is the guy who kicked off the blood sausage tradition and now presides with good-natured efficiency. "What we have here is a mixture of barley, onions, and certain other ingredients," he says with disconcerting vagueness, unscrewing a half-gallon jug—when the blood glugs out in a dark wave. If you haven't shaken hands with your new friends yet, forget it: in five minutes everyone is forearms-deep, ladling and cramming the mixture into casings of pig intestine. It looks like mass murder. "This is all about Christmas," Vanaselja reminds us. "This sausage represents our traditional meal, what the holidays are to an Estonian."

"Estonian blood sausage" sounds like a dire exotic, but Vanaselja's wife Aili (it's her recipe) points out that most pastoral cultures have a variety, from *morcilla* in Spain, to Irish black pudding, all the way to Bhutan, where it's made with rice. When you take part at the Estonian House, you're enacting a harvest rite with unfathomable roots. And of course you can eat and drink here during the rest of the year (some hours are members and guests only—so make a friend). New York Estonians have a quality common among displaced populations: an understanding attitude toward strangers. If you show some interest, you'll be immediately and warmly repaid. Start with this: "*Rōōmsaid Jōulupühi*"(Merry Christmas).

PHAGWAH IN RICHMOND HILL

- Early spring; see website for info: www.phagwahparade.us
- Transport: A train/Ozone Park – Lefferts Blvd

> **The springtime Hindu festival of colors**

Holi is the festival of colors that takes place on the Sunday after the first full moon of the Hindu calendar. It's named after Holika, an unkillable demoness in the Vishnu-worship tradition. Here we could have a lengthy and fascinating discussion of Indian myth; know that in the end Holika got burned to ash, and to mark the impossible event, people throw fistfuls of vivid powder at each other. The festival coincides with the beginning of spring: color triumphant.

"We call Holi 'Phagwah' in Trinidad and Guyana!" shouts a middle-aged woman, one of thousands of people lining 125th Street. Most of the Hindus in the Richmond Hill area of Queens are from those places, and seemingly all of them have come out to fill the sidewalks as a parade of neighborhood dignitaries rolls past to blasting music and rolling drums. "There are many kinds of Hindus, but this is the victory of good over evil, so it doesn't belong to any one tradition! I have to get you," she adds with a serene smile, and slaps a handful of bright blue powder in your correspondent's face. A young father keeps an eye on his son, who has already been stained a deep primordial hue as he darts at knee level with a water rifle loaded with purple dye. Asked if Phagwah is a good way for New Yorkers to get to know the Indian community, the man nods happily. "It's a good way for *me*. I live in Brooklyn. Some of these people I haven't seen for years."

The parade makes straight for the best-named of all New York City's parks, Smokey Oval. Here the music reaches concert decibels, and anyone with asthma or critically dry skin should think twice. The more or less civilized powder-bombing from the street becomes a roiling frenzy, with plumes and gouts of glitter and sprays of liquid color. The good sports become unrecognizable smears, like they've survived a happy calamity: they puff rainbows as they whirl around. When the sun comes out, it lights up low-hanging clouds of pastels.

The point is to dive in and get dirty. On the subway you'll get increasingly interested stares as you head back to wherever you live, and for a while you'll be fascinated every time you blow your nose. The muddy swirl down your shower drain might as well be winter itself, spiraling away … and gone.

BOCCE AND ITALIAN ICE

William F. Moore Park
Bordered by Corona Avenue, 108th Street, and 51st Avenue
• Transport: 7 train/103 St – Corona Plaza; Q23 bus/108 St – Corona Av;
Q58 bus/Corona Av – 51 Av

> **A double of classic Queens**

Where Corona Avenue meets 108th Street you'll find the small wedge called William F. Moore Park by the official map, and Spaghetti Park by everybody else. It's the place where you can indulge in a double of classic Queens. First, a stop at the Lemon Ice King of Corona (at 52nd Avenue), where the ices have been made according to the same standards and fresh-fruit recipe for nearly seventy years—truly the undisputed best in the city. The question of where to eat it is answered by a sanded court in the park set up for bocce, the Italian game where grapefruit-sized balls are rolled or pitched at a smaller target ball, and egged on by a lot of yelling. Eating ice and watching bocce in Spaghetti Park has a kind of landmark status in this neighborhood: it's as much ritual as activity.

The park, historically Italian, is now in flux, according to the tireless New York process of culture flip. The immigrants today are mostly Latino; at the bocce court's shaded table sit several men: Colombians, Ecuadorians, Hondurans. Some wait to play, others grow quietly buzzed on Coca-Cola and vodka. On the court an older Italian man, Nico, is defending a vanished status quo against a young Mexican. Nico shoots overhand and racks up twice as many points as his opponent with apparently half the effort. The reigning ace, though, is a Dominican everyone jokingly calls Obama because of a passing resemblance. After casting, he flattens his hand and glides it like a wing while he fixes the departing ball with a hard stare, as though controlling its trajectory from a distance. Weirdly, this seems to work. Obama's fast pitches crack like gunshot; his slow balls creep to exactly the right spot, and stop. Asked what his trick is, he shrugs and smiles—exactly the answer you'd expect from a bocce genius.

During the day bocce seems to tend to be more of a men's club, but at night—reversing the usual pattern—the families come out. At some point, some inspired citizen strung Christmas lights over the court, giving the strip of packed sand the homey excitement of a carnival midway. Sitting on a bench with a lemon ice and taking all this in, you might wonder how, where other places are nowhere spaces, Spaghetti Park got it right.

THE INTERNATIONAL EXPRESS

MTA 7 train

Welcome to everywhere

People come to the city from countless places for countless reasons; a fair number of them end up in Queens. It isn't just the most ethnically diverse urban area in New York—it's the most diverse anywhere. This is convenient for the person interested in the world and the different people in it: you just have to cut right through the borough on the 7 train, dubbed the "International Express."

Get off about anywhere east of 33rd Street. The neighborhood of Sunnyside is a mix never intended by geopolitics: Romanians, Turks, Greeks, Irish, Koreans. It's not all harmony. "Too many Muslims," a storeowner from Bucharest shakes his head sadly. "Colombians hate Venezuelans," says Emily (mixed South American heritage). She waits with her friends (Dominican, Argentinian …) in front of a movie theater. "But you interact with different kinds of people," she says, "and learn different situations." Tolga, a Turk smoking a cigarette as he waits for his turn at a barber shop, says, "I like it, actually. It's more interesting. Like a …"—he searches for the term "melting pot"—"… like a *culture soup*."

Hispanics are a constant along the 7 line, particularly on the south side of the tracks, until the last stop at Main Street: this is Flushing, one of the city's "other Chinatowns" (see page 239) and every bit as vividly Asian as the original. Along the way you can pass small efflorescences of community, for instance 69th to 71st, which is Filipino. Argel, a middle-aged Manileño with a bristling black mustache and a frame that fills his XXL tee-shirt, has a philosophical attitude about other cultures. "If they don't mess with me, I got no problems. If they do"—he juts out his belly and reveals a surprising amount of eye-white—"watch out." The greatest mind-bender is the neighborhood of Jackson Heights. Turn north on 74th Street for a blast of the Subcontinent. Indian women in patterned saris, Bangladeshi women with covered hair, Pakistani women peering through the eye slit of full *niqabs*. Silver-bearded Sikhs are stationed along the sidewalk in front of jewelry and clothing stores. You've got boutiques, and street hawkers, and bakeries just like anywhere in the city—but the articles aren't from here. The very air seems imported.

FLUSHING CHINATOWN'S GOLDEN MALL

41–28 Main Street, Queens
- Hours: 10:30 am –11 pm
- Transport: 7 train/Flushing – Main St

> *A little place for noodles and New York City for good taste*

Flushing's Main Street is crowded, and teeming, and deeply foreign, and its capital seems to be a marvelous warren of shabby restaurants in a basement. This, the Golden Mall, is fronted by a worn archway with half of the steel lettering busted off; the first floor contains a few restaurants, a shoe vendor, a computer shop, and a telecom outfit. But discover the stairs (you have to go back out again), and you'll descend through, apparently, some sort of bewitched portal to mainland China. It's the first test. The second is finding a seat in this maze: there are a dozen food joints in the mall, each smaller than the other, each accommodating a gang of far-flung immigrants. What a Westerner calls Chinese food, you may have suspected, is modeled to suit Western expectations. Here you get the other thing.

"Try this," says a woman from Hong Kong who calls herself Kat. She sits at one of the six chairs crammed around tiny tables in front of Lan Zhou Handmade Noodles, and motions with her chopsticks at a stainless-steel pot. What is it? "Something that makes the soup hot. It's good, but," she cocks her head, perhaps searching for the term "nerve damage." This chili sauce, which everyone spoons onto everything, turns out to be the kind of hot that gets gentler in the second act after some of your brain has steamed out. The noodles are whipped up on a countertop about 3 feet wide: a column of dough is swung, and doubled, and swung, and redoubled, and finally chopped up and thrown into a boiling pot. The soup is simple, hearty, delicious. "'A little place for noodles,'" says Noah in the next chair over, translating the Chinese symbols on the wall, "'and New York City for good taste.' It's from Gansu province," he adds. "Not like Chinatown food—that's too sweet!"

Next it's a stool at Tianjin Handmade Dumplings, where a dozen cost three bucks. A couple of Taiwanese friends share a plate, dipping into a dish of chili and soya sauce mixed with vinegar. "This is like a night market, we have in every China city," says one. "You can get all kind of snakes." What he wanted you to hear was "snacks," but with "Lamb Offal Soup" and "Hot and Sour Sausage Fun" on the menus, you start to expect anything. A pile of meat the uniform color of boiled beef is labeled "Duck Heads"—lean in and that's exactly what they are. "I cut in half," says the man, "and eat the brain. Often a tongue in there." Make a note for next time.

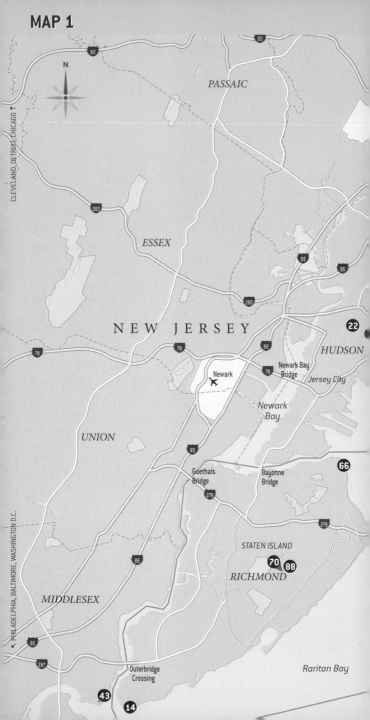

MAP 1

MAP 2

WESTCHESTER

BERGEN

George Washington
Bridge

38

46

62

BRONX

86

Harlem

Randall's
Island

Central
Park

✈ La Guardia

Lincoln
Tunnel

NEW YORK

MANHATTAN

Midtown

Queensboro Bridge

29

QUEENS

103

105

Queens Midtown Tunnel

Flushing
Meadows

41

42 **79**

3

64 **13**

East River

Hudson River

39

Holland
Tunnel

71 **93** **25**

Brooklyn
Heights

NEW YORK

Downtown

102

7

Governors
Island

33

98

berty Island

Prospect
Park

pper
Bay

BROOKLYN

21

John F. Kennedy ✈

azano-
ows Bridge

KINGS

Gravesend
Bay

Jamaica
Bay

44

wer
ay

Coney Island

35

32

60

**ATLANTIC
OCEAN**

0   5   10 km

MAP 3

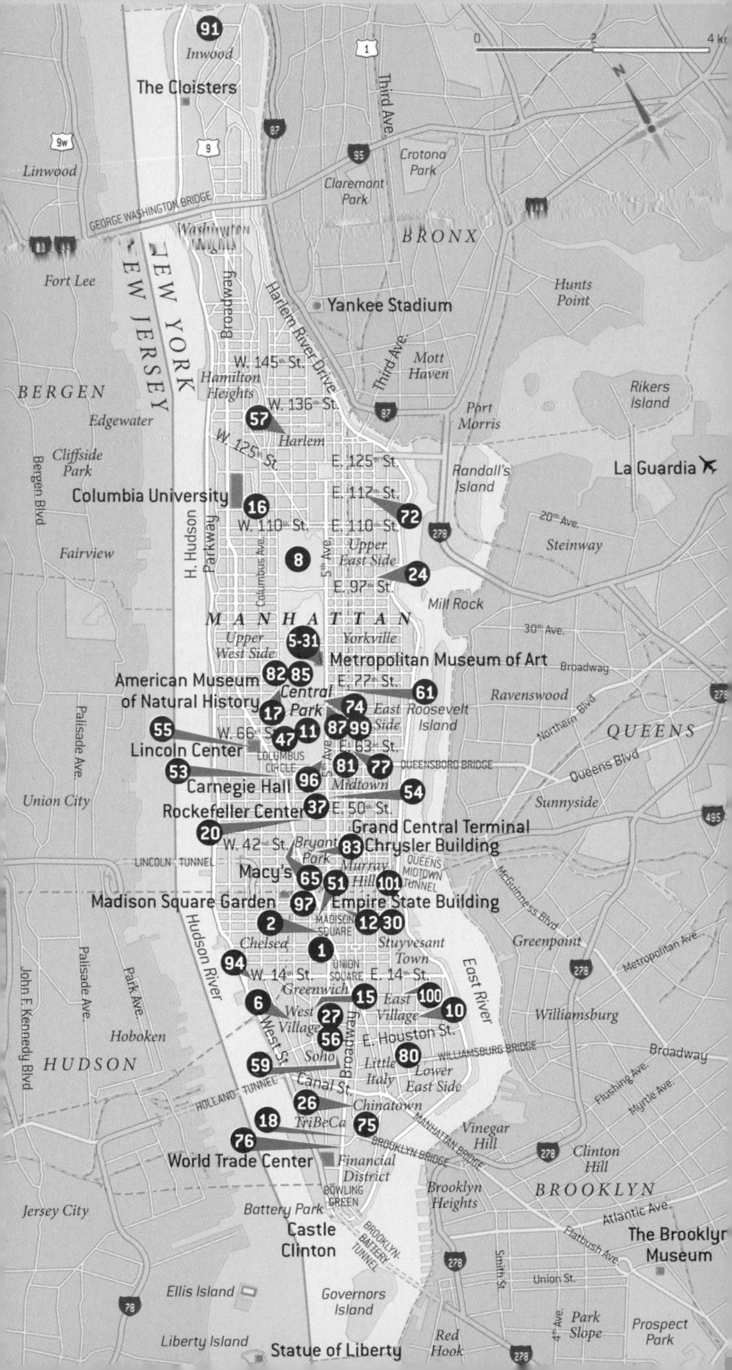

91
Inwood
The Cloisters
Linwood
George Washington Bridge
Washington Heights
Fort Lee
New York
New Jersey
Broadway
Harlem River Drive
Third Ave.
Crotona Park
Claremont Park
Bronx
Yankee Stadium
Hunts Point
Mott Haven
W. 145th St.
Hamilton Heights
W. 136th St.
Bergen
Edgewater
57
Harlem
W. 125th St.
Port Morris
Rikers Island
Cliffside Park
Bergen Blvd
E. 125th St.
Randall's Island
La Guardia
Columbia University
16
E. 112th St.
72
W. 110th St.
E. 110th St.
20th Ave.
Steinway
H. Hudson Parkway
Columbus Ave.
Fairview
8
5th Ave.
Upper East Side
24
E. 97th St.
Mill Rock
Manhattan
30th Ave.
Upper West Side
5-31
Yorkville
Metropolitan Museum of Art
Broadway
82
85
American Museum of Natural History
E. 77th St.
61
Central Park
Ravenswood
17
74
East Side
Roosevelt Island
Northern Blvd
55
W. 66th St.
47
11
87
99
Queens
Lincoln Center
Columbus Circle
E. 63rd St.
Palisade Ave.
53
81
77
Queensboro Bridge
Queens Blvd
Carnegie Hall
96
Midtown
54
Union City
Rockefeller Center
37
E. 50th St.
Sunnyside
20
Grand Central Terminal
W. 42nd St.
Bryant Park
83
Chrysler Building
Lincoln Tunnel
Murray Hill
Queens Midtown Tunnel
Macy's
65
51
101
McGuinness Blvd
Madison Square Garden
97
Empire State Building
Hudson River
2
Madison Square
12
30
Chelsea
1
Stuyvesant Town
Greenpoint
Metropolitan Ave.
94
W. 14th St.
Union Square
E. 14th St.
East River
Palisade Ave.
Park Ave.
Greenwich
15
East Village
100
John F. Kennedy Blvd
6
West Village
27
10
Williamsburg
West St.
56
E. Houston St.
Hoboken
Soho
80
Williamsburg Bridge
Broadway
Hudson
59
Little Italy
Lower East Side
Flushing Ave.
Myrtle Ave.
Holland Tunnel
Canal St.
26
Chinatown
18
TriBeCa
75
Manhattan Bridge
Vinegar Hill
76
Brooklyn Bridge
Clinton Hill
World Trade Center
Financial District
Bowling Green
Brooklyn Heights
Brooklyn
Jersey City
Battery Park
Atlantic Ave.
Castle Clinton
Brooklyn-Battery Tunnel
The Brooklyn Museum
Flatbush Ave.
Smith St.
Union St.
Ellis Island
Governors Island
4th Ave.
Park Slope
Prospect Park
Liberty Island
Statue of Liberty
Red Hook

ALPHABETICAL INDEX

ALPHABETICAL INDEX

NOTES

NOTES

Acknowledgements:
Thanks to fellow adventurers and kind strangers.

Photography credits:
All photographs by **T.M. Rives** except Judd House (Anita Shah).

Maps: **Cyrille Suss** - Layout design: **Roland Deloi** - Layout: **Stéphanie Benoit** - Proofreading: **Jana Gough**

© **JONGLEZ 2014**
Registration of copyright: April 2014 – Edition: 01
ISBN: 978-2-36195-076-7
Printed in France by Gibert-Clarey
37 170 CHAMBRAY-LES-TOURS